L, Ploriel

PLOUGHSHARES, a journal of new writing, is guest-edited serially by prominent writers who explore different and personal visions, aesthetics, and literary circles. PLOUGHSHARES is published in April, August, and December at Emerson College, 100 Beacon Street, Boston, MA 02116-1596. Telephone: (617) 824-8753. Web address: www.emerson.edu/ploughshares.

EDITORIAL ASSISTANTS: Darla Bruno, Gregg Rosenblum, and Tom Herd.

POETRY READERS: Paul Berg, Brian Scales, Michael Henry, Renee Rooks, Charlotte Pence, R. J. Lavallee, Tom Laughlin, Bethany Daniel, and Ellen Scharfenberg.

FICTION READERS: Thomas McNeely, Billie Lydia Porter, Emily Doherty, Michael Rainho, Leah Stewart, Tammy Zambo, Monique Hamzé, Karen Wise, Holly LeCraw Howe, Andrea Dupree, Scott Clavenna, Jessica Olin, Jeffrey Freiert, and Mary Jeanne Deery.

SUBSCRIPTIONS (ISSN 0048-4474): $21 for one year (3 issues), $40 for two years (6 issues); $24 a year for institutions. Add $5 a year for international.

UPCOMING: Spring 1998, a fiction and poetry issue edited by Stuart Dybek & Jane Hirshfield, will appear in April 1998. Fall 1998, a fiction issue edited by Lorrie Moore, will appear in August 1998. Winter 1998–99, a poetry and fiction issue edited by Thomas Lux, will appear in December 1998.

SUBMISSIONS: Reading period is from August 1 to March 31 (postmark dates). Please see page 230 for detailed submission policies.

Classroom-adoption, back-issue, and bulk orders may be placed directly through PLOUGHSHARES. Authorization to photocopy journal pieces may be granted by contacting PLOUGHSHARES for permission and paying a fee of 5¢ per page, per copy. Microfilms of back issues may be obtained from University Microfilms. PLOUGHSHARES is also available as CD-ROM and full-text products from EBSCO, H.W. Wilson, Information Access, and UMI. Indexed in M.L.A. Bibliography, American Humanities Index, Index of American Periodical Verse, Book Review Index. Self-index through Volume 6 available from the publisher; annual supplements appear in the fourth number of each subsequent volume. The views and opinions expressed in this journal are solely those of the authors. All rights for individual works revert to the authors upon publication.

PLOUGHSHARES receives additional support from the Lannan Foundation and the Massachusetts Cultural Council.

Retail distribution by Bernhard DeBoer (Nutley, NJ), Ingram Periodicals (La Vergne, TN), and Koen Book Distributors (Moorestown, NJ).

Printed in the U.S.A. on recycled paper by Edwards Brothers.

CONTENTS

Winter 1997–98

Cover painting: *Blueberries with Clothespin and Pine Cone* by Susan Walp
Oil on linen, 8″ x 8″, 1996

Ploughshares
Patrons

This nonprofit publication would not be possible without the support of our readers and the generosity of the following individuals and organizations. An additional list of donor acknowledgements may be found on page 231.

COUNCIL
Denise and Mel Cohen
Eugenia Gladstone Vogel

PATRONS
Anonymous
John K. Dineen
Estate of Charles T. Robb
Scott and Annette Turow
Marillyn Zacharis

FRIEND
In Memory of Larry Levis

ORGANIZATIONS
Emerson College
Lannan Foundation
Massachusetts Cultural Council

COUNCIL: $3,000 for two lifetime subscriptions, acknowledgement in the journal for three years, and votes on the Cohen and Zacharis Awards.
PATRON: $1,000 for a lifetime subscription and acknowledgement in the journal for two years.
FRIEND: $500 for a lifetime subscription and acknowledgement in the journal for one year.
All donations are tax-deductible.
Please make your check payable to
Ploughshares, Emerson College,
100 Beacon St., Boston, MA 02116.

Introduction

I like songs I can relate to," Ray Charles said in an interview in 1960, long before "relate" became part of the ubiquitous psychobabble. And I guess that was Jane Shore's and my one persistent criterion for the work we've included in the following pages. In some fundamental, surprising, persistent way, the poems and stories announced themselves and stuck with us on first reading, or else we came back around, until subsequent readings finally instructed us how to get purchase on them. So there it is, simply put. The pleasure of reading; revelations born of rereading. Obviously, too, this was our rare opportunity to offer a compendium of contemporary (with the exception of Jonathan Galassi's splendid translation of Eugenio Montale) writing, whose depth, amplitude of earned and rendered emotion, and outright craft impressed us. Each accepted work had to have some inimitable sense of integrity and immediacy and permanent fix on the world, of course, because how else to judge? Editing, furthermore, gave us a special, humbling sort of experience: publishing writers whose writing lives have now spanned at least four decades: Joyce Johnson, Philip Levine, Hettie Jones. There was the counterpoint excitement, too, of introducing newer writers— new to us, at least—such as Lily King. In my case, the editing hours allowed me to admire my wife Jane Shore's tough-minded, generous sense of discretion. I read the fiction, Jane read the poems; indeed there was little consultation about final choices. And that seemed right, because whatever level of competence we felt we suspected would implement itself most successfully in that exact division of labor.

Jane observes, "I found I had chosen poems that had the sound of the human voice. What do I mean? They sound like a person talking, but in heightened language, telling me something urgent. And most of these poems, in retrospect, tell stories about people—mothers, children, husbands, even literary figures: Keats, D. H. Lawrence. They struck me as fresh and unpretentious.

I didn't plan it this way, but when ordering these poems for the magazine, they seemed to speak to each other, toss ideas and arguments back and forth amongst themselves. Reading these poems is like being in a room with a group of fascinating and lively people. One wants to eavesdrop in on their conversations, and then jump in."

I recently served on an NEA panel for fiction, nonfiction, and translation (right in Washington, D.C., far from home in Vermont). In between cordial, heated, always rigorous panel sessions, I'd cab over to listen to various Congressional harangues (and witnessed a few in private offices), myopic assessments, and, on far less frequent occasion, passionate advocacies for arts funding in America. Imagine, if you will, the exhibitionist spectacle of a tax-paid representative waving a volume of so-called "pornography" (which actually was a collection of brilliantly subdued erotic stories), eyes turned to the ceiling, as if that was the one partition between him and God, imploring, "Why should we support this smut?" The sheer level of intellectual violation was at times mind-boggling. At night, I could not help but return to work on this issue of *Ploughshares* with profound happiness (mitigated, of course, by the dire forecasts of what might happen to the individual artist's grants, funding for magazines, etc.). But happiness, nonetheless, I admit, for the most selfish yet familiar and sustaining of reasons: I was back in my room, which was full of light and all these passionately forged words on the page—many pages. And able to sit for consecutive hours, working. Philip Roth put it this way: "Writers live mostly in a room." Editors do, too, I guess.

Compared to many, I have not taught writing workshops for very long. I have no working philosophies about the phenomenon itself. But I had one student, at the University of Maryland the first year I taught there, in 1988, named Ernest Acosta. He was Cuban. He died of AIDS some years back. Now and again I reread his splendid novel, *Second Exile,* which he completed shortly before his death. Anyway, Ernie would sit in the workshop, his intense, handsome face a mask of well-rehearsed torments, when only an hour before, over a coffee, he had presented only the upmost serene sweetness of person. He'd listen to what was read, or whatever critique of a story was offered (he never went first), and when it was his turn to comment, he'd often begin with a profound sigh of resignation. He'd loosen his collar. "Is it just me, or is it suddenly hot in the room?" He'd rub his face like kneading bread dough, work up to a statement, often replete with a kind of anecdotal philosophy. Here's an actual example: "Well, I *suppose* we're all here for a reason. Maybe even the same reason. It's to ask, Does this writing have *soul*? If it doesn't, we shouldn't be bothered; we should be drinking a cold glass of water, putting the glass to our foreheads and feeling great relief we no longer have to suffer through this." It was melodramatic, sure—even preposterous. But it saved us all a lot of extraneous babble, especially the inept investigative strategy I was so amateurishly wont to overuse that year: "What's the writer's ambition here? Is it the right ambition, and if so, how well-executed is it?" I relied on Ernie. Because he cut out all the in-between bullshit and went directly to the *useful* idea of writers upping the ante, writing at the top of their capacity at every given moment, and of being *uncompromising*. He took writing *personally*. So, that's one other thing I felt about the poems and prose in this issue (written by pros, many who've had hundreds of writing students of their own); reacting to them, Ernie Acosta (my ghost editor) would not have sighed, gone out for a smoke, mumbled in Spanish something incomprehensible but nonetheless frankly indicting—no, he would've said, "All right. Now, we have something I'd like to *memorize*."

I feel pleased and obligated to mention Jane Shore's long association with *Ploughshares*. In 1977, Jane edited the poetry for Vol. 3, Nos. 3&4, which she refers to as "The Elizabeth Bishop Issue." And she edited again, with Ellen Wilbur, Vol. 10, No. 4, in 1984. She first met the founders, DeWitt Henry and Peter O'Malley, in 1971—so her association goes back quite a ways. I thought about *that*, and about the prolific generosities of *Ploughshares*, when witnessing arguments for and against the support of literary journals on Capitol Hill (I can't get those NEA "debates" out of my mind). I guess it would be accurate to say that *Ploughshares* is a literary community whose good writing has helped keep, as Joseph Brodsky said in a lecture once, "anesthetizing despair at bay." Because without good writing, despair is what, I firmly believe, we would fall victim to.

I used to keep a kind of daybook: odd jottings, letters never sent, desperate ideas for anthologies, quotes, etc.—useless, really. But I at least *felt* like I was working. One obsession was to chronicle other writers' reports, notions, suggestions of what Peter Handke, in an essay by this title, called "A Successful Day." I had entries from Peter Esterhazy, Junichiro Tanizaki, Bashō, Wallace Shawn, Beckett, Mandelstam, Virginia Woolf, Jean Rhys, Kerouac, Paul Blackburn, Miklos Radnoti, Boleslaw Sulik, Cees Nooteboom, and so on. My long-term intention was to construct a consensus profile of "The Successful Day" in a writer's life. It was a nonsense project; it kept me busy. In the end, most accounts—tucked into journals, letters, occasional pieces, even novels—had little to do with actually writing. It had to do with walking by the sea, talking on the telephone, buying light bulbs, fretting over illness, seeing a matinee, endless driving, fixing a bicycle, dinner with friends, love—anything but owning up to the inescapable (thank our lucky stars) *preoccupation* that is writing. And one day in New York City, I actually saw my all-time favorite writer, Max Frisch, in the Gotham Book Mart. I couldn't believe my luck. It was far more thrilling than seeing—well, to me—*anyone*. And, reader, I confess to actually following him. Out of the bookstore. Through the diamond district. He walked blocks and blocks, smoking a pipe. He was dressed in a casual suit, sensible shoes. I followed him for maybe an hour. He bought a pretzel. He went into a bar and drank a beer. Finally, he went into a small uptown hotel. *To write,* I thought, to carry on with *a successful day.* But actually I doubted it, because he had bought a dozen magazines en route. I mention all of this because one unexpected reward of editing this issue was an uncanny kind of *connection* (however self-serving) with the writers in this issue, some of whom Jane and I know personally. I fairly obsessed in trying to imagine, in all their various cities and houses, what their working days were like: perhaps comprised of not writing, but at least *thinking about what they are writing*. A diary of a writer not writing would be a far cry from a book about "writer's block"—pray tell, we don't need any more of *those*.

That is all. Editing has allowed us to be in residence with fine writers, the chance to reminiscence, to guess at the nature of other writers' lives, to read all sorts of things we might not have otherwise. We thank all of our contributors for sending their work.

GREGORY ORR

Best

The Greeks said: never to be born is best;
next best, to die young in a noble cause.
"Où sont les neiges d'antan?" Villon asked.

"Where are yesteryear's snows?" is, I guess,
the phrase in English. Villon spoke in praise
of women not born when the Greeks said: "Best

not to exist at all." Yet the French poet pressed
on with his list: great beauties of the past.
"Où sont les neiges d'antan?" Villon asked.

In his great poem, only their names persist:
Joan, Beatrice, Blanche of the White Arms.
Were the Greeks right: not to live at all is best?

What would Blanche's lovers say to this
who are themselves just dust, all suffering
long gone as the snows after which Villon asked?

Beauty is like life itself: a dawn mist
the sun burns off. It gives no peace, no rest.
"Où sont les neiges d'antan?" we ask.
But the Greeks were wrong: to live and love is best.

The Alternate

I had to ask someone how to find the criminal court building, so apparently I'd led a sheltered life. A woman directed me to Franklin Street and said I couldn't miss it. I walked east toward the hulking gray walls which dead-end that part of the city. It was the cold Monday after New Year's. No one had shoveled the snow or put any salt on the ice.

I'd spent the entire holiday alone. For ten years, as long as I'd been seeing Michael, that was the way it was. All weekend, I'd stayed in the apartment. When the year changed its digit, some drunken boys shouted in the street, and one driver beeped his horn. Then all the sounds were the usual.

Frankly, I felt glad I'd been called to jury duty. A number of times, I'd managed to evade it, but I'd used up my last deferral. At the moment I could think of nothing I'd rather be doing, though I remembered to complain about the awful inconvenience whenever I talked to other people. Being a juror seemed a blameless way of using up the next two weeks. After that I would have to look around for something else.

In smaller cities I've seen courthouses that look Jeffersonian, white columns that make you think of justice. The criminal court building was Deco, but not my favorite kind that reminded me of the World's Fair. This kind of Deco I'd call penitential, with its heavy straight lines and its narrow windows that look barred from a distance and its base of filthy brown marble and its entrance that is somehow like a giant latrine. Still, as I've said, I didn't mind having to go there. It was like travel to a foreign country. There was even a border crossing before they let you on the elevators, where they combed through your bag and checked your body for concealed metal. You rode up to your floor surrounded by muggers or drug dealers, who stood aside politely to let you off.

I'd hoped to get on a jury right away, but there were three days of waiting. I wasn't prepared to wait so long. The emptiness threatened the feeling I had of being temporarily becalmed for reasons that had nothing to do with my own choices or acts. The room where they made everyone sit was enormous and overheated and had about three hundred blue plastic chairs. The name of each person present went into a brown metal drum. There were long periods of absolute tedium, then the drum was spun around, and the clerk started reading off names. He was a man with white hair and a cop face, and when he called your name over the loudspeaker, you had to rise immediately from your seat, take everything you owned, and walk into a smaller room to await instructions about your destination. It was all determined by chance—both where you would end up that day and the fate, perhaps, of a defendant. The clerk said no one was to take it personally if your name wasn't called or if you weren't selected as a juror. Yet each day as the room would empty more and more and those on each side of me would rise and go, I couldn't help feeling I had been overlooked or passed over for reasons I couldn't understand. It was as if even here the old pattern of coming very close and being deflected was operating.

I was trying not to think of the Michael situation, so I struck up a conversation with the young blond woman next to me. She was a nervous wreck because she had just left her husband. She had an eight-month-old son and feared she might get sequestered. Every now and then she'd pull photos of the baby out of her bag. "Did I show you these?" she'd ask. On our second day of jury duty, we went out for a Vietnamese lunch in Chinatown; when we came back, the clerk called her name, and I never ran into her after that.

When you think of people who have gone very suddenly out of your life, what often comes to mind is the last time you saw them; you go over all the details in amazement, each one sharp, drawing a little blood. What amazes you is that there will be no next time. I see myself walking down Michael's block quite astonished that I'm actually doing so, yet moving forward nonetheless. And the ironically festive setting, the wreaths and the lights in the windows of the brownstones. I feel quite light myself, almost disembodied. I float right past his house since it isn't at all familiar to me. I just know the number, the fact that he lives on the second floor. I walk back two houses and see a dim yellow glow behind the second-story shutters. I almost don't press the buzzer. When I do, one of his children answers, and I say who I am, thinking that now none of this can be undone. No one buzzes back. Instead Michael comes down the stairs and flings open the door. There is a look on his face he has never shown me, even in the worst of times. "What are you doing?" He can hardly get the words out.

"*Henshaw!*"

It was the third morning. The sound of my name over the loudspeaker brought me up short. This time I wouldn't get to complete the scene, analyze the look, wonder if I was mistaken. I scrambled for my coat, my newspaper, my handbag, and stumbled gratefully toward my assignment. I soon found myself in a corridor on the thirteenth floor.

There were no benches in any corridor of the criminal court building, and none of the drinking fountains worked, and the judges were never ready to receive the prospective jurors. I learned all this from an indignant elderly man who offered me a piece of hard candy as we leaned against a wall outside the courtroom. Many of our group had sat down on the brown marble floor, not even caring about the dirt. Our crowd of weary jurors soon resembled an encampment of homeless people. Everyone agreed that this treatment, the lack of the most basic amenities, was a disgrace. The man with the bag of hard candy was convinced that all the original benches had been removed so that the real homeless would not invade this building in search of places to sleep.

When the door to the courtroom finally opened, we filed in and collapsed into all the seats on the left side. I had a good view of the defendant—a young, husky, light-skinned man with a thin mustache curving unpleasantly down over his mouth. Behind him sat a red-haired woman, her chair pulled up very close to his. He'd lean his head back, his eyes slightly closed, and she'd whisper into his ear, her lips almost grazing the side of his cheek. At first I wondered if she was his lover, and if she, too, would be on trial. But it turned out she was only his interpreter. The defendant, Luis Benitez, who had shot his common-law wife, Ysidra Delgado, in the belly with a .44, didn't understand a word of English. His lawyer was making the plea that Luis Benitez had been suffering from extreme emotional disturbance at the time and was therefore not guilty of first-degree murder. In an old French movie, it would have been a *crime passionel*.

The judge asked if there were any of us who for personal reasons felt we could not serve on a jury for this trial. There was practically a stampede of people asking to approach the bar; most got sent away with satisfied looks on their faces. Very few wanted to deal with a killing. Personally, I didn't feel fazed by the idea. To tell the truth, I very much wanted to get on this case, to occupy my thoughts with Luis Benitez and Ysidra Delgado. With each person who left the courtroom carrying their coat, my chances improved. When the brown drum was spun around for the last time, I had a prickly feeling that my name would definitely be one of those it yielded up.

"*Henshaw!*"

I walked to the jury box and took one of the fourteen seats.

The judge and the lawyers wanted to know about each of us and whether we had ever been crime victims. I said I was divorced, no children, a freelance graphic artist, that I had lived for the past fifteen years on the Upper West Side, and once had my purse stolen on the IRT. When the judge asked had I ever experienced domestic violence, I recalled something I had almost forgotten—a ludicrous scene at the end of my marriage when I hurled a wooden bowl full of onions at my husband and missed. "No, I haven't, Your Honor," I answered, also thinking of the last time I saw Michael, though not a blow had been struck by either of us and we'd never shared much domesticity, apart from the Chinese takeout we'd sometimes ordered in. There was only that look of his that I couldn't mistake—Michael always sticks his tongue in his cheek when he's about to boil over—and a very brief exchange of words before he backed away and shut the door:

"What are you doing?"

"Walking around." And I shoved the shiny shopping bag into his hands. "Merry Christmas!" I more or less assaulted him with the mini cappuccino maker and a little card on which I'd written, "Only connect!" I would still like to know whether it ended up in the garbage.

I was curious about why I was not selected to be a regular juror for the Luis Benitez trial, but merely one of the alternates. Was it the defense who distrusted me, or the prosecution? Was it the wrong inflection in my voice—"No, I haven't, Your Honor"—or was it just plain mathematics?

The judge said some diplomatic words about jurors who came down with the flu and alternates being absolutely essential to the whole process. It reminded me of the way a married man will string you along by his need of you, so that for years you feel the situation will change eventually.

"Lucky you," said one of the regular jurors afterwards as we rode down in the elevator. "At least you won't get sequestered out in Queens with the rest of us. They won't put us up at the Plaza, that's for sure."

On the first day of the trial, the prosecutor opened a carton containing the outfit Ysidra Delgado was wearing the day Luis Benitez shot her. It was a two-piece black-and-white-checked suit, over which she'd worn a nylon ski jacket, pale pink with an ugly cream yoke. He took each separate piece out to show to the first witness, giving it a little salesman-like shake so that it would fall properly. The suit looked child-size, so Ysidra must have been a thin, tiny person; there were gold buttons down the front of the jacket and red braid sewn around the pockets, but the beige fabric was ugly and cheap. I realized after staring at it that it was a knockoff of a Chanel. I guess Ysidra put it on because it was Easter, and now here it was, all torn apart the way the EMS people had cut it off her body, except someone must have laundered it because there wasn't a trace of blood.

The witness gasped and looked tearful. "Yes, that's Ysidra's," she murmured.

I noticed Luis Benitez leaning so far forward in his seat that his interpreter practically slid off her chair in her attempt to reach his ear. The outfit no doubt brought Ysidra back for him, maybe the live Ysidra as well as the dead one. Suddenly he turned his head, and his gaze became directed at the jury, specifically, I felt, at me.

I immediately focused on the witness, a woman who made her living by "helping a lady." She used to find ladies for Ysidra to help. "Me and her, we were like sisters." She didn't think the relationship between Luis and Ysidra had ever been good, though they had lived together seven years. Ysidra was too old for Luis, who was now only thirty-one; she had left two sons in Dominica who were almost grown men by the time she brought them to the United States. The sons didn't want Luis around, and a few weeks before he shot her, Ysidra had kicked him out after a terrible fight. After that, the friend said, Ysidra had been afraid to leave the house. Still the friend had persuaded her to go to church with her on that Easter Sunday. When the two women left the church, they saw Luis waiting outside in his parked car. The friend told Ysidra to run, and she ran into the bodega across the street, but Luis had seen her and got out of the car with a gun in his hand.

The prosecutor passed around pictures of the vehicle taken from several angles—you could just make out the cement steps of the church through the side windows. Some of the jurors held them for a long time, as if they contained some hidden clue. The car was a black livery cab, the kind you see all over the West Side in the mornings, the kind I used to take when I worked in offices and would oversleep after Michael's visits, always being careful to settle the price before I got in. Luis could have been one of my drivers, one of the ones with a crackling radio and a folded newspaper on the front seat. I would never have imagined that the newspaper concealed a gun.

Did Luis Benitez carry the .44 with him all the time? Or did he wake up on Easter Sunday with a plan, just as I did that Saturday morning before Christmas, staying warm under the covers for a while with the idea that seemed to have flown into my brain overnight? The idea of buying the gift and of taking it to Michael. Wasn't that in the spirit of the holidays, wasn't it the way people like us should treat each other? It seemed that with one gesture I could say everything. Whenever I was with Michael, words always gave me great difficulty. "Tell me what you want," he'd demand, "speak," but only when he meant I should suggest some variation in our lovemaking.

I went out to Broadway that morning and found a gift that wouldn't look too personal, in case friends of Michael's were there besides his kids. I convinced myself he would ask me to come in, though part of me didn't think so at all. It was his first Christmas without his wife. I'd always thought he would eventually leave her, but instead she'd left him. He got to keep the kids until New Year's while she was in the Bahamas with her boyfriend. So Luis had his gun, and I had this German cappuccino maker that supposedly produced perfect foam, all nicely wrapped up with a red bow inside a big shopping bag—also the card that I've mentioned.

On the second day of the trial, we were shown more photos—these of the bodega where Ysidra had taken refuge. You could see bullet holes in a freezer and an aisle where merchandise had fallen off the shelves—bags of potato chips, cans of various things. There had been a great change in Luis—maybe his attorney suggested it. He had shaved off his mustache overnight. His real face was round and babyish, rather sweet, actually, not one a woman would have run from. Had he grown the mustache to look older for Ysidra Delgado, more worthy of her respect? Was the gun he carried into the bodega another stage prop for him? Was he too afraid of rejection to confront her empty-handed?

Luis and the victim had often stopped in at the bodega. The owner was the star witness. He had seen everything, the shooting, Ysidra Delgado's blood on the clean floor of his shop, the cans of Goya beans crashing down with her falling body. He was fat, and he perspired, talking so agitatedly in Spanish that the red-haired translator, who had now positioned herself near the witness stand, would sometimes ask him to repeat what he'd just said. When Luis's lawyer raised questions about some of his testimony, he insisted that Luis had spoken to Ysidra in an absolutely normal tone of voice. *"Normal, normal!"* He waved his hands in fury when the lawyer professed disbelief.

They kept going over what Luis had said to Ysidra. "Come out to the car. I want to talk to you." Luis Benitez just kept saying the same thing—"I want to talk to you. I want to talk to you"—never raising his voice, everything still *normal*. I thought how angry you could be in a normal voice, how you'd struggle to keep it level so there'd be no telltale tremor. You'd want to show the other person you're not affected by them, although it's true you want to talk. Ysidra didn't want to. They never do. But all you're asking for at first is time—enough time to reach the right combination of words.

Ysidra tried to get past Luis to the door. He blocked her path. She ran into the aisle full of canned beans and potato chips. There was no way for her to escape. At the end of the aisle was the freezer Luis fired into before shooting Ysidra in the belly. He told the police the gun had dropped out of his hand and gone off accidentally. The police knew this was impossible.

We had to be shown the murder weapon. I held it for three seconds, surprised it was so much heavier than it looked. Then came the bullet taken from Ysidra. The bullet was nothing, junk—a little piece of useless metal about the size of a Hershey's Kiss. We passed it along from hand to hand.

I'd never fired a gun in my life, not even in an amusement park.

Before dismissing us, the judge told us the case would wrap up tomorrow, and that we'd better come in with our suitcases—all of us, even the alternates. That night I packed as if I was going away for a holiday weekend, although I doubted I would be going anywhere.

My fellow jurors were an ill-assorted lot. There was nothing to talk about except Luis Benitez, who could not be talked about at all. The weather was awful, so there was conversation about ice. The youngest juror was always late, so people made jokes about him. He was a musician from the East Village who obviously stayed up all night. He once asked me for half of my tangerine.

On the final morning, the regular jurors suddenly bonded. They had all brought in food. The table in the jury room was covered with candy, bagels, bananas, tortilla chips, ginger ales. The court officer was taking orders for free delicatessen sandwiches, because no one would be allowed to go out for lunch. The musician, who was a vegetarian, had to settle for lettuce and tomato on rye. Everyone felt sorry for him. "Have *two* sandwiches, hon," one woman said.

Luis's shirt was black that day; around his neck hung a crucifix. When the interpreter whispered in his ear, he didn't seem to listen. He was staring at the jury, at each one of us, scared and imploring. I wondered if he would remember our expressionless faces.

Before the summations, his lawyer called only one witness—a psychologist who talked about how Luis Benitez had wet his bed after his mother had abandoned him years ago in Dominica. The prosecutor said that was irrelevant; the judge sustained the objection.

I kept thinking that if Ysidra Delgado had only agreed to listen to Luis Benitez, she might still be alive. That when she ran from him, he didn't know any other way to reach her. And the gun made everything too fast, too irrevocable. If the bullet had missed, he might have continued uselessly hoping she'd take him back until the hope finally wore itself out.

I guess I would have tried to explain this to the other eleven jurors and held out for a lesser charge than murder in the first degree, but I was only an alternate, and the judge told the alternates they would no longer be needed. He thanked us for performing our civic duty, and we even got our free sandwiches.

I left the criminal court building and walked out into the empty afternoon, stepping on ice all the way to the subway.

I did something late that night I'd sworn to myself I wouldn't do. I picked up the phone and called Michael. "I've been on jury duty," I told him, as if I was returning from a long trip. "And I've been thinking. Isn't it crazy for us not to talk about what happened?"

"You want what you want," he said.

We never spoke again.

LORRIE GOLDENSOHN

Seven Bullets

The bullets took their thuggish way,
and like words once sounded
couldn't be unsounded.
Was I like him?

Very sadly, with immense
and quiet bitterness one by one
the blood members of your body—
daughter, grandson, and granddaughter—
have heard you say
I should never have married him,
thereby unsaying us.

Small and excitable,
he beat you when drunk, drank
when he lost a job, and then sober again,
caressed his infant daughter, me.

A German girl, down on her luck,
you brood in the houses of the rich
in which you serve.
One couple hires you, themselves
in the throes of separation.
At night, nanny and housekeeper,
you pad up and down the stairs,
the husband bent over the piano—
What you need is a nice quiet divorce,
he says, Schumann's *Waldscenen*
streaming under his fingers.

In six months you hope to be free
to marry again.
My Filipino father cannot dissuade you

from the man you choose in his stead:
in the only snapshots left
he is a tombstone with a German name,
he is a lineup of people
in riding clothes, blond
in that sepia light, he is
thin-lipped, smiling, and elegant.

Fritz who knows horses: among the file of riders,
he sits on one, mouth open
to speak the familiar words
in the language for which you thirst.

Somehow he acquired a riding stable over here,
and then, in that blind, unlucky trustfulness
apparently part of his gallantry,
he loses the horses to a friend
who sells them behind his back
the year his mother's sickbed calls him home.

Even after Fritz was shot because of you,
this grieving mother
poured such healing into her letters—
until the bombing raids over Bremen
stopped them. For so many years
she called you her "daughter."

In the months before Fritz,
you sewed for one family,
and still a novice, coached by my father,
cooked badly for another;
and then you keep house for Mrs. B.

In 1937 a hopeful Fritz returns to America,
and starts over as her groom.
And there, digging the ballpoint pen
firmly onto the onionskin pages
you write for us, the descendants,
how you met him, over two fine riding horses:

Of course I had to see the horses,
of course we had the same interests,
that was being home again, and a cultured man,
polite and attentive to me...

But first there was my Filipino father.

Alone together, I think,
in that square old Studebaker,
who knows down which country road.
My father driving and uttering threats.
He took out the gun,
and waved it in your face...

But you write that you didn't believe him:

I was a girl well-brought-up—
this was not what could happen to me.

It shakes him:
the pistol in her face, and even then,
his ruddy, fair-skinned German wife—
pound for pound no doubt his match in weight—
talks down the barrel of his will,
her voice passing right through
and melting it.

My father. He used to play the "ukelelly."
He stole the boss's liquor
and put his feet up on the table.
The envy of his friends,

he let you go out and work, staying
at home for bootleg gin
and making those delicate drawings...
We grip our pencils—I, too,
make my cross-hatched
velour-shaded mark in ink and soft lead,
and sing in the shower when happy,

though unlike me,
my father cannot carry a tune.

The seventh child of farmers,
he spoke Spanish, a "dialect" probably Tagalog,
and an English better than yours.

Fritz, pink—or Fred, tawny!
Unable to face the double-barreled sequence
of my father's Spanish name, you banished
his race and called him Fred:

Fred was the butler from the other apartment.
When I got stuck with something,
he would come in the kitchen and help me,
and when he heard footsteps
he would run out quick as a wink.

Of course, I was very grateful for that.
I must say again I was lonely,
and for my actual years
far less mature as I should have been.
It felt so good to lean on somebody.
Fred got me out of trouble
when I got myself in it.

Fritz should never have gone with me,
you say. *If he had not been there*
I could have talked to Fred,
just as I did that day in the car.

What did you ever understand?
Indignant at the "fleabags" Fred took you to,
at the nice hotels and good restaurants
whose waiters would not admit you with him.
Once he brought you to the burlesque.
He was not educated, you say,
in such amazement.

Mrs. B. discharged you, afraid of Fred.
He will hurt you, she said.

But my mother, closed in her private war
between the wars, stayed in the mess being made:

The German men, who stiffened when they saw
the German girl dating her Filipino man—
wanting to "protect" you—
and Mrs. B., threatening deportation—
writing nasty letters to your brother Joe.

All those things made me just more stubborn.
Embarrassed, frightened,
you went out with my father and his friends,
all the men carrying their hidden knives.

On our day off, we would see a movie,
have dinner in a dirty little hole in a wall,
and I missed what I took for granted
in Germany very much.

I try not to blame you. Had I been friend
instead of daughter, I would have told
my stocky, pretty pal with the stubborn underlip,
the one in the photo wearing the bathing dress,
to drop this man.

White silk, and sprigged with strawberries,
her bathing dress slipped coolly through my hands
grasping at photos, all
folded within the satin paisley
lining the steamer trunk from Krefeld;
the trunk, smelling of camphor and lavender,
chosen with such
particular care:

Papa's only daughter,
clutching her worthless Weimar currency,
running her errands and pausing
before the red shoes in a shop window.
In the morning, desiring them,
she promised to return
with a suitcase full of money—but by noon
the price had risen to two suitcases full of money.

At some point—brooms, cartons,
and a dump truck—none of your doing,
all of your doing, took the whole lot
into ashes or festering landfill.

At night, it yanks me bolt upright, sleepless,
gritting my teeth, furious
at the losses, those you suffered
and those you provoked—photos and lace,
steamer trunks, rings, and letters—letters.

Fifty years later I speak to you directly.
For the first time I put a question
and do not wait for you
to bring me something, and then, squirrel-like,
run off to stash it with the other puzzling bits.

You answer with the simplicity of the dying.

Once again your brother Joe takes you in.
Don't go home, he tells you.
At the cottage where you've moved
to evade my father, Joe finds the ashes
warm in the grate, a note from Fred on the table,
promising to be different, promising
to hang on to you through death ...

Stay where you'll be safe, says Joe.
His first idea—as guard or witness?—

to send his ten-year-old home with you,
into that flashfire of wills and blood.

But arm in arm with Fritz,
on you come from New York.
He only intends to go with you
as far as Hillsboro, where you drink a Coke.
There is so much baggage—
all that goes with a twenty-two-month-old baby—
he decides that he'll help you to the platform.
He is so sure he is coming back
he leaves his hat in the station café.

Then on the platform a change of heart.

At nightfall, the two of you at Joe's farm.
The little cousins give up their spaces
to make room, and not yet a couple, you are led
to a chaste sleep in single beds.

In the morning, the drive to the lawyer
to see about divorce.

The house so full of your comings and goings...
To my aunt, you are the wayward sister
unsuitably shedding her unsuitable man;
with angry fear and rank impatience
she greets you coming back,
to warn the two of you that Fred is here,
and has a gun. You write:

I shrugged it off as nonsense.
Fred came a short time later.
He wanted to speak to me.
Fritz said, I come, too. We were
hardly seated, he pulled the gun out,
screaming, When I cannot have you, nobody else will.
He aimed at me, Fritz

jumped in front of me
and got that shot in the head.
He died instantly.
Fred kept on shooting.
I got three, one that went
through the lung and shoulder, two in my hand.

There is a baby suspended on your lap, unharmed.

Then the gun jammed. People came.
People put me on the porch floor,
I was bleeding terribly—
all of a sudden there were so many people—
and one brought me to the Great Barrington hospital.

I did not care if I died or not.

The onionskin pages are so incomplete.
There were seven bullets in the gun,
you told me yesterday,
the talk between us finally urgent
as you settle your affairs
and almost ninety-two, make ready to depart.
Seven bullets and three shots,
and then the gun jammed.

But you miscount: the bullet in Fritz
you count as your own, Fritz an afterthought,
because Fred was aiming at you.

My mother rushing across America
to meet my father's gun . . .

I, too, some miscounted part of you,
some part of him,
and of the man who died;

in other, disconnected talk, caught
in the rasp of competing memories—

the gun jams after my mother falls,
and as I am taken from my father's arms
my aunt says to him,
"See what you've done."

Where were my father's arms,
where and for what were they taking me?
Holding me, and aiming the gun at his temple?

If I could say to my father,
Just put me down.

Overnight

All the familiar contours chasten.
The lake is a pool of dark thought.
There, the clouds bear pale change,
gathered in contemplation.

The lake is a cup of gray fear:
your body in the cold dawn
upturned, and my own drowning eye
opened on the floating light.

And I can see the pines unclasp
each from each, and the sky
rising a little, and always the world
under its leaf of gold.

And I can hear the black ice take
around the island's certainty,
and my own voice, and a pair
of loons unmooring in the mind's ear.

Man at the Piano

"I had known him as a child
when he played guitar: thin,
hyperactive; with a clear soprano then.

Later, the golden curls had straightened
and grown dark. He played nothing now
but of a doubt so broad his family feared for him:

Talent like that drives the nails in, they said,
although it was the world he hammered out
as when he entered me it seemed the source

of all knowledge had been displaced. More curse
than song. More freedom from remorse, in him,
that longed to give up self-love to desire,

but meant: to have been bound by nothing,
     like a photograph,
the black and white of him his skill protected
a mood more fundamental than the song itself.

While my one art, for which he'd blame me still,
despite the years it's taken to uncomplicate
that touch of his, which had reviled flesh

so fully as it took the place of music,
is that I've never known how to forget
that history of his: how song

once followed him; rained down
and filled him from a high cloud: Knowledge
like a cleaving. Amnesty I would not grant."

Another Republic

*Existence can only be justified
from an aesthetic perspective.*
—Nietzsche

When we come upon the hawk for the first time,
I am reminded of the line by Cézanne,
the landscape thinks itself in me
then imagine a current of sunlight for the bird,
the aerial pencil sketch of nearby meadows
and woods, the light hysterical.

My neighbor caught the red-tail with a gloved hand
when the bird spun into his workshop, flight confused,
feathers to wall stunning itself against a windowpane.
Talon, beak, square white breast, dappled brown, big as a cat.
Called to come see this wild thing, anyone would think of
hunger and the imperceptible movement in the grass.

All the neighborhood children are in a circle
surrounding the cage when I leave.
There is a branch, a swatch of old carpet,
a towel covering the setup.
I tell my daughter to walk straight home
after the bird is fed, tagged, and released.
The trees are leafless, married
to rivers of damp shadow.

The sky is that diluted blue—
that accompanies bright light, reminiscent
of when the watercolorist drenches the sheet
and blue blurs by degrees to white.
Dense old growth dwarfs the spackle
of the short ornamental flowering trees.

I think of the bed of feathers, twirled reeds,
the perch and vision afforded by the swaying
upper-story of the tallest trees.

A while later I see my little girl running,
big coat unbuttoned, open, flying toward home.
When she enters the kitchen she is out of breath,
reports all that was left in the end was,
the fat little gerbil's head,
the little gold seeds from its belly.
She walks with purpose toward the black piano,
throws the red coat to the floor and plays
the classical solos memorized
till there is a space, a blue quarter of sky
between herself and the awful order of things,
what is devoured, the gloved hand, the hooded eye,
the bird's hunger. The music
is a curtained window which contains the great beyond
and she plays like a dog runs—
it does not know what it is doing
but it equals distance.

Infant Joy

L. infantia, *inability to speak*

I hear your infant voice again,
unspooling on a tape made years ago—
No, though it was paradise, I can't,

can't go back to that room, filled
with your rounded vowels, the sighs
and crooning of a newborn child,

bright syllables strung, like beads
on a string, into meaningless meaning.
One night, as you slept,

I read Blake's song:
I have no name:
I am but two days old.

By a circle of light, I read,
exhausted, stunned:
What shall I call thee?

And you, in a dream
beyond me, cried out:
I happy am, Joy is my name.

You laughed the laugh of creation.
Beyond the darkened room,
a framing radiance, beyond

the framing radiance, the world.
But for an everlasting moment,
we were there, *together,*

in a place such as Blake knew,
your infant syllables dissolving terror,
fear, all that could befall me, you.

Meaningless meaning made new!
Sweet joy but two days old,
Sweet joy I call thee . . .

And I was laughing, too,
to read Blake's song.

The Scan

We were given these instruments after your birth:
syringe, Tegaderm, Heparin flush.
This morning, I found them behind the file cabinet.
Dare I throw them out?
I am a superstitious girl.

When I stood in the parted door and gave you up
for the scan, anesthetized, dye-injected,
your one-year-old body sang
its sweet, green galaxy of bone.
In the corridor, children sat tethered to IVs,

one in a party dress, incongruous as her lack of hair.
Slumped in your room's black corner,
I thought: nothing can save us,
unbelievers. I am not like Abraham,
ready to make such a sacrifice.

Yet a voice entreated:
Come with me—just this far.
I went to the cold, metal table,
where you lay in the dark.
Haven't I always taken care of her?

Isn't she still here?
When I looked,
I had to say yes,
even as the clicking machine
aimed at your chest.

Girl at Thirteen

At the end of the dark at the end of the hall,
my older sister stood by the mirror,
casting for her real face in a square of light.
I was eight. Had she known that I was still awake,
pillow doubled under to raise my head,
she'd have screamed and slammed the bathroom door,
but she never caught me watching.

Night after night, whether I was up or sleeping,
Diane rehearsed her repertoire of grown-up looks—
frank astonishment, disdain, excitement, ardor—
working all the moving parts: the wide-set laughing eyes,
blue-gray under arched brows; the strong mouth,
its lower lip beveled flat as our father's;
the broad Gentile nose and high cheekbones;
hair pinned onto rollers, tight as a row crop . . .
but in the mirror it was free, and she was Princess Grace.

Early that fall, my father switched our places
at dinner one Friday night.
He'd caught her vamping in the mirror
while he was singing Kiddush.
Since then, she'd sat in my chair—
back to back with her own image, wild tips
of dark-blond hair glinting in the Sabbath light.

From the darkness of our crowded room,
I loved to watch the one-act show.
Diane would brush her teeth.
She'd shut the cold water off and run the hot
before opening the blue jar of Noxzema.
Waves of mint and menthol issued down the gloomy hall
as she dipped and dabbed the cream

onto cheekbones, chin, forehead—circling and circling
as if it were fingerpaint, her skin the shining paper.
Then she'd splash her flushed face clean
and pat it with a soft gray towel.

She turns to me, a nameless girl,
and reaches for the switch.
I hear her slipper hit the creaky spot
outside our bedroom door.
She slides by in her nylon nightgown,
pulls back the covers of her matching twin.

The radio crackles on.
Wispy siren ... static, then cheering—
a baseball game, the Senators going past the ninth?—
the announcer's voice exultant, too low for me to hear:
the sounds of chance roiling like seduction in her ear.

JOYCE PESEROFF

The Dress

It wasn't lewd or revealing
of anything round except my
shoulders which Mother forever
urged back with military brio,

yellow—never my best color—
a square of magenta for the bust,
bought in the Village at mod,
expensive Paraphernalia (what

Grandpa called his bait and tackle;
his paraphernalia). Did you know
that store? Glossy white go-go
boots and skirts a palm's width

of outlandish fabric—foil, or fur.
This was fine cotton, faux-
Courreges/Mondrian (that square)
and spaghetti straps my mother

sighed over. So wrong for me!
I clung to the dress—I almost
said, like death. A neighbor,
summoned to arbitrate, fist

tight beneath her chin,
concurred. What else—break rank
with a mother's need to steer
her child? What swells awaited this

flimsy cotton kayak of a dress,
what rock but the stone of opinion
rattled against adulterer
and whore. But not for me. For her.

That I'd wear such an ill-looking
dress spoke ill of her. She'd failed
to teach me. Style and taste, acquired
through years of shopping discount,

wholesale never retail (Paraphernalia!
techno-lettered shopping bag
I returned to West Fourth, my hip
life scuttled): lore meant to live

within me, where Grandpa's tales
of frenzied feeding bluefish whirlpool still—
after he'd given up on all sensation,
hating food, light, fresh air (a draft!)

a shut-in whose sheets abraded him,
elbow to ankle, whose cheek
couldn't bear the pressure of a kiss.

The Death of Schumann

Celestine Truxa was born in Salzburg on the eve of Metternich's coronation as prince. According to the midwife, her mother split up the middle like a birch tree hit by lightning, managing to stay alive just long enough to see her daughter's face lodged in the crook of her husband's arm, eloquent of birth and glistening, before she died.

It's unlikely she died content. Celestine's father, Oswald Truxa, was a suspicious man by nature, though often thought credulous and kindly, due to his dull-witted expression and his enormous size. Almost seven feet tall, he could lift Celestine clear off the ground, whirling her like an angel above his head, even after she'd passed her twelfth birthday and such activity was no longer deemed appropriate. "Can you see him, my little mousie?" he would demand, as Celestine watched the upturned and politely noncommittal faces of the townspeople slide past, to be replaced by what she believed were the faces of the drowned, floating to the surface of the River Salzach in globes of light. Around and around her father would spin her until, finally, she would tilt her neck back to see over the wall of rock called the Monchsberg, and up into the sky, which was, generally, bright blue. "The fiend's arms are long, mousekin, but he won't get you. So long as there's breath in this body," Oswald Truxa would yell, "he will never lay a hand on you!" Oswald Truxa was a revolutionist, and the fiend he had in mind was, of course, Metternich.

Always, in that first moment as she felt her feet leaving the ground, Celestine would experience a combination of fear and delight. It was so wonderful to see the world from the air! But what if her father were to let go? Even while she felt his big fingers gripping her waist, she worried whether it could happen that she'd begin spinning too fast, wrenching loose, rising higher and higher until the whole world would shrink to the size of a button, and she'd find herself approaching the terrible face of God. For, the truth is, it was God to whom she thought her father was referring. Still, even from so high up, she could see the bottle-green heads of the ducks swimming on the Salzach; she could smell the sweet pomade her father used to make his hair lie flat. Soon, she knew, they'd be sitting together on the riverbank, tossing crusts of stale bread to those same ducks. The ducks would quack, and her father would try to amuse her by quacking back.

When he wasn't plotting the overthrow of the Holy Alliance, Oswald Truxa worked as an artisan, carving toys that eventually found their way into the nurseries of the aristocracy. He was not an imaginative man, but his paranoia made him attentive to detail, and so his creations were in great demand. On any summer day you might see an intricately carved white horse with eyes of lapis, drawn on its silver-spoked wheels among the rosebushes of Mirabell Castle behind the retreating figure of a boy or girl— the enemy's plump, unblemished offspring.

Celestine adored these children, though her adoration was that of the bird on the wing for its bright reflection in the window-pane; she didn't understand the tremendous gulf between her life and theirs. After all, didn't she, too, own a circus wagon with gilt bars, out of which she could lift a tiger painted yellow and black? Not to mention the sly dancer named Loona-Maroona, whose jointed legs spread to accommodate the back of a star-spangled elephant. Because they were presents from her father, Celestine tried not to notice how the elephant's tusks were cracked off at the roots; how the dancer's legs were comically short in proportion to her torso; how the tiger's gaping mouth was toothless. But by the time she was willing to admit to herself that her father's presents were nothing more than those toys rejected by his more discerning patrons, it was too late. The habit of adoration had been formed, altering only to suffuse the reflected image with the light of religious significance. Celestine came to believe, then, in the perfection of innocence, towards which she strived as if it lay ahead of her, as if the flower moved, inexorably, from the dissolution of late summer back to the green, stirring heart of the bud.

It is no accident that such a young woman would have flourished in the very town where Paracelsus not only lived, pursuing his alchemical career, but where he also died of metal poisoning. Nor is it an accident that she would choose to sit at the foot of the statue the town fathers erected to his memory; almost every afternoon she could be found seated primly on the convenient wrought-iron bench, her large hands folded, pale white, in her wide dark lap. And, whereas Oswald Truxa sought anonymity—together with a growing band of revolutionists he maintained a hideaway in the rocky outcroppings beyond town—Celestine craved such attentions as might come her way in the manner of mice, skittering through the rooms of a vast house, locating on the sideboard in the pantry a crumb of blue-veined cheese.

So it happened that one afternoon in late August a soldier came to sit beside her on the bench. The nighthawks were beginning to stir on their ledges, all at once, like the dark appendages of a huge, reviving organism, its mute intelligence visible in the manifold lights of its eyes. But whether those eyes were lit from within—the hausfrau rising on tiptoe to set a match to the wick—or whether it was the effect of the sun going down behind the Monchsberg, spilling its gold across all the windows of Salzburg, Celestine couldn't tell.

The soldier was a slim man of indeterminate age, his bones sharp, prodding through folds of weather-darkened flesh. On his head he wore a cap with a beak-like visor, from under which his hair flew out in pale filaments; his eyes were the shade of blue the whey assumes, dripping from the curd through the meshes of the basket. Celestine immediately understood that he was a foreigner, possibly of Nordic extraction; that the whiteness of his hair might indicate age, or experience with terror, or merely an extremity of blondness. His uniform was a baked brown, deeply rucked and furrowed, like the banks of the river in seasons of drought. If he carried a weapon, she couldn't see it. Was he a mercenary? The single medal he wore pinned to his narrow chest was in the shape of a fish, and bore no resemblance to any token of bravery she'd ever seen before.

Years had come and gone since the last time Celestine oscillated like the needle of a compass above her papa's head. She was middle-aged—an old maid by the standards of the day—and already, at thirty-five, beginning to show signs of the deafness that would inform with heavy irony the final years of her life; those years spent in service to the great musician Johannes Brahms, whose melancholy harmonies worked their way as if through cotton batting into her brain, where they suggested nothing so much as the

PLOUGHSHARES

unintelligible whisperings of her father and his cohorts, through the thick plaster of her childhood bedroom wall. Still, her vision was excellent: indeed, Celestine had retained her ability to imagine the world from an elevated point of view. If she could see the Salzach's flow darkening beneath its several bridges, could she also see all the way to Vienna, where revolutionary armies were converging, her own father among them? Could she see Metternich as he watched his pretty maid sneak a sip of wine from the decanter? Could she see him set his napkin fastidiously across his lap, only just considering flight to England?

It was not unusual during such periods of upheaval to find soldiers in unfamiliar costume wandering around the streets of Salzburg. Still, there was something about this particular soldier that made Celestine uneasy, though it must be admitted he'd in no way displayed any of the grosser characteristics associated with his kind. He sat at a respectful distance on the bench, staring toward the river with a look of comprehensive gloom; his hands rested on thighs which, Celestine couldn't help noticing, were, taken together, scarcely as wide as one of her own.

"It's been a long time," the soldier finally said, "since I have found myself in a landlocked place." His speech was polyglot, yet strangely elegant, as if not only had he spent his life traveling from country to country, but immersed himself in nomadic scholarship as well. "It is difficult to breathe in such places, is it not? I have always thought that would account for the monstrous size of your countrymen's rib cages."

"I've lived here my whole life," Celestine said.

The soldier nodded his head and smiled thinly. "You're Magyar, am I right? The black eyes, the clavicles a man might grab and row like oars. Forgive me. I've been among savages so long, I've forgotten nice talk and sweet words. I am a man of honor," he asserted. "Don't be afraid."

"I'm not," Celestine said, but she was lying. A shiver poured through her body, like a shiver through the hide of a ruminant, jerking loose flies. "Where are you from?" she asked.

"If you mean where was I born, it was at the very tip of Jutland, in a town called Skagen. An ugly place. Still, children are perverse. They'll love anything. And I was seduced with my first breath. It was the damp salt wind of the sea, which I've been hungry for

44

ever since. Among the Lapps, in the Finnmark, the flavor is more strongly of fish; on the island of St. Kilda it's like when you stick a cut finger in your mouth. In fact, I spent several years on that island, leading what people refer to as the monastic life. Which merely means I spent several years feeling bored in the presence of a higher being. Do I shock you?"

"I don't think God is boring, if that's what you mean," Celestine said.

"You've probably never been forced to think about him twenty-four hours a day," the soldier said. "In any event, it was on St. Kilda where I happened to study the writings of the man standing above us. Which is why I can't help wondering whether you've got some reason for sitting here. Or are you, like so many of your sex, without the curse of purpose?"

No one had ever asked Celestine such a question before, and she realized—as she felt breaking in half, deep within her chest, a round smooth stone; a stone such as she'd found when she was a child, which her father cracked open with a hammer, revealing inside a turreted, crystalline city—that she was not an ordinary woman. She almost cried out, the pain was so sharp, her exhilaration so intense. "But I am cursed," she said. "Only, it's difficult to describe. Sometimes," she said, closing her eyes, trying to locate her heart among all those crystal buildings, "I watch other women walking with their children along the river and I can't imagine what it would be like. Would it make me happy to have a child?" Celestine paused. She thought her heart was the size of a seed, but very beautiful. "It's never seemed to me that it would," she said.

"People in this country waste too much of their energy on pro-creation," the soldier said. "Paracelsus had the mind of the land-locked. It's not surprising he came from such a place, where men spend their lives prying from the integral alp bits and pieces of this and that. Do you understand?"

Celestine smiled. "But I've heard it said that this very place where we're sitting was once covered by the sea. That's why there's so much salt buried in the rock, and why little children picking cloudberries sometimes find the skeletons of whales high in the mountains."

"On St. Kilda," the soldier said, "a man will say 'I doubt' when he means 'I believe.'" He turned in a single, rigid motion to face her directly.

Celestine felt her fear of him close its hand around the little seed of her heart. He looked so much like one of her father's clockwork toys that she found herself wondering at what moment, and by what invisible agency, the key had been twisted in the aperture. How carefully her father would lick the tip of his brush into a point, before painting in the pupils on a doll's eyes! The soldier's eyes were terribly bright, and his pupils like the tips of pins.

"I doubt," he said, "that you have ever known love. Maybe you're biding your time, waiting for its arrival? Maybe you think it is a singular event, just as Paracelsus thought God was a singular being, extruding primary matter the way a spider extrudes silk?"

"I'm waiting for no one," Celestine said. She watched the lamps being lit along the banks of the river, the flowers of light blooming on the river's surface, like the lily-covered barges that would float there during the Feast of Corpus Christi. From far off came the sound of gunfire as, across the square, a young girl flung open a casement window and leaned far out, her face a white, featureless disk, her arms extending, arbitrary, toward the sound.

"That's what I'd hoped you would say," the soldier said. He stood up and took Celestine's hands in his own. "It was only a matter of waiting," he said, drawing her up from the bench. For the first time, he looked surprised. She was so tall.

"My father," she said. "He'll wonder where I am." And then she shrugged. "But he never has before," she added drily. "He's a soldier, too."

In fact, Celestine was taller than the soldier by a head, and she had to make a conscious effort to shorten her stride—the stride of a woman accustomed to walking by herself—as they passed in silence along streets that became increasingly dark the farther they got from the center of town. The air, likewise, acquired intensity, filling in with the cold exhalation of stone.

"Now you must climb," the soldier at last said. Courtly, he held back the branches of a fir tree, and Celestine could feel the tree's new growth stroke her cheek, its scent entering her nostrils and tunneling directly upward to a place behind her eyes, where it set off a strange, ocular jingling. Was it possible the path they climbed was composed of ants and bees? Was it possible the soldier's hand was a single star in an immense constellation she was about to enter? At first, alder bushes clutched at her skirts; in time, they were replaced by cushions of moss and veins of running water.

Celestine had never felt this way before: the outer part of her body having become the brittle housing for a substance alternately fluent and concussive that she decided must be her spirit. The floor of the cave into which the soldier led her was spread with bedstraw, so with each step her sense of division grew stronger, unable as she was to reconcile the sweet, milky odor of a meadow with the moist and decomposing odor of this hole where he apparently made his home.

"It goes on forever," he said, "and then it falls away. Come here," he said softly, and Celestine surprised herself by moving toward him, toward that opening shaped like an O which he locked in place over her own lips, creating a chamber into which her spirit entered eagerly, to be lapped up little by little all night long. In the morning she was astonished to see how noiselessly the sex had retracted back into the soldier's body; he sat fully clothed at the mouth of the cave, boiling coffee over a fire of resinous wood. Sunlight washed around his feet, over Celestine's thighs and belly and breasts, filling her with apprehension.

"The fighting's started," the soldier told her. "Now we'll find out if Paracelsus was right." He pointed across the plain to where isolated puffs of smoke rose and dispersed, turning the pale blue sky a rosy brown, the precise color, Celestine thought, of the secret parts of her body. For the first time she noticed a rifle, leaning against the wall of the cave. " 'That which is above is one with that which is below,' " the soldier said. "Or so Paracelsus wrote. Do you think that means God was corrupt when he made this world?"

"No," Celestine said. "I think God acted out of innocence."

The soldier lifted the rifle and squinted along the sight, aiming at a squirrel that ran—first partway up, and then partway down—the trunk of a stunted pine tree. Whenever the squirrel stopped, it jerked its head straight to the side, rotating it all around on the fluid joint of its neck, as if it wanted to be watching at the moment of its own death. "Do you love me?" the soldier asked.

"I don't know," Celestine said, and then she hesitated, wondering. "Yes," she said, finally, "I think I do."

The soldier put the gun down, and stood up. "Then you should come here and kiss me goodbye," he said. "And when you think of me, it will be as if I'd set out in a little boat across that sea of yours that used to cover this place, that filled all the hollows of this cave with its restless body. I expect I'm about to die for a cause to which I'm entirely indifferent. Do you think if I had shot that squirrel, God would have wept? Still, I don't think it would be a bad thing if you were to weep for me. Those of us who've lived our lives where the world breaks apart into sand and salt and millions of drops of water know that the only immortality is conferred by the terrible human heart."

In the years to come, even during the brief period of her marriage to a kindly and reliable man—a cheerful man, with whom she came to understand the thin boundary between happiness and boredom—Celestine nursed her memory of that night with the soldier, conjuring it by whatever means were available to her. Her pincushion, for instance, was filled with balsam fir needles; she kept a collection of small stones in a bowl on her bedroom windowsill, and when she was alone she would sprinkle the stones with water, close her eyes, and inhale that strict and mineral odor. The smallest stone she occasionally sucked like a lozenge.

This was Celestine's secret. Certainly her husband wasn't aware of his wife's private dreaming: her external manner had altered with the years, settling into a kind of ironic good humor he misconstrued as solicitude. But the truth is that even on their honeymoon, as she walked hand in hand with him along the shadowy esplanade of Gmunden, watching the swans' necks curve like question marks above the Traunsee; even as she sat with him in the hotel dining room, nibbling the swan-shaped vanilla ice cream, prodding loose the sliver of candied orange peel that was the beak with her spoon— even then, Celestine was remembering the soldier.

Eventually, she and her husband had two children—a boy and a girl—and though she knew it wasn't possible, at certain moments Celestine thought she recognized in her daughter's delicate bones the soldier's likeness. She named the child Thule; the little boy was called Max, after his father.

Oswald Truxa survived the revolutions of 1848, and his last act was to make each of his grandchildren a special toy, in each case bearing out their specific instructions. Max requested a circus bear, large enough to ride; Thule, despite her grandfather's attempts to convince her that a pretty, life-sized doll would be more appropriate, insisted on a wooden man. Nor would she allow Oswald to give the figure moveable joints. "I want him all in one piece," she said, "like a stick." Every night she took the thing to bed with her. *My Baunchie,* she called it, and Celestine had seen her waving it around in the darkness of her room, speaking for it in a voice that sounded like a nail being drawn from a board. "No, Papa," Thule would say, sitting bolt upright whenever her father tried to pry her fingers loose from the figure as she slept. He was convinced it would bruise the satiny skin of his daughter's arms and neck, incapable of recognizing a strength of purpose greater than his own.

Within a single year, Celestine lost both her husband and her father. Each of the funerals took place on days of intense clarity: the skies were cloudless, the freshly dug earth almost black, the grass around the grave, on one occasion, pale green and tender; on the other, concealed by thick patches of campion and rosebay. Thinking back, Celestine realized she could not remember which funeral was which. The priest's words had been the same, the collection of mourners similarly garbed and solemn. On both occasions Max had cried as if his heart was breaking, and Celestine recalled how she'd realized that his loss was the most complete— that he was now consigned to a life without advocacy, whereas Thule's spirit appeared suddenly rampant.

They moved to Vienna, to a large apartment on the third floor of No. 4, Karlsgasse. This was a middle-class residence in the style of the late Empire, the vestibule stained red and blue and yellow as light seeped in through the panes of the French windows. Returning home from school in the late afternoon, Thule liked to submerge herself in each color, assigning titles to her days: "Today I am a blue girl," she would announce to the world, and the world would respond with a soft intake of breath.

At night, Celestine would tuck her children in, and then give herself over to their separate bedtime rituals. Max liked stories involving a series of obstacles over which a hero—characterized by goodness of heart and simplicity of demeanor—triumphed. Because he allowed Celestine complete control over her narratives, in time she came to understand the relationship between plot and will. It was as if a metal armature insinuated itself within a spongy knot of details, like the beanstalk up which young Jack climbed, the smell of his blood thickening the atmosphere, clotting here and there into events.

Thule, on the other hand, insisted on complicity, and her passion was for the mutable. She always wanted the same story, but she wouldn't tolerate a predictable outcome. Originally, Celestine had been the storyteller, but little by little Thule took over, and Celestine could no longer remember the precise moment when the words ceased to come from her own mouth, and began to emerge from her daughter's. Or was it the *Baunchie* who spoke? Celestine could never be sure. Thule had outgrown her habit of clutching the doll, but it remained propped on a chair in the corner, surveying the room with its bright, nutty eyes. Whatever its source, the story Celestine listened to, night after night, was the story the soldier had whispered into her ear, so long ago, as she lay curled on her side, each small movement releasing the frothy sweetness of the bedstraw. And, though in its unfolding the story was always different, it always started out the same way:

"Once upon a time," Thule would begin, "there were four sisters who lived all alone at the tip-end of the universe, where the sea licked up the sand their house was built on a grain at a time. They had no mother, but they all remembered the day she left. The wind was blowing like crazy, and they could smell the breath of dead sailors in the air. As they watched they could see their mother running away from them; her feet were going up and down, and her arms were whirling around and around like windmills."

"But," Celestine would sometimes remind Thule, "don't forget that Fortune was with them. Remember? For while we all know that Fortune is a woman, she is definitely not, my heart's darling, a mother."

Because Thule took delight in the unexpected, she tolerated such interruptions, though she never really understood what her mother was talking about. "I *know*," she would reply. "I just forgot to say that part." And then she would go on to describe how the first sister liked to sit with her feet in the sea, watching them disappear, watching the sea draw with its many small hands a coverlet of sand over her toes. "It's a gray day," Thule would continue, "and the sky is like the big hood of a bell without a clapper. The first sister is perfectly happy sitting and listening to the sound the gulls' feet make landing on the rotten wood of the pilings. She's thinking about what it's like inside the house. She can see how the wind blows the door open, and how it picks up the edge of the lace tablecloth. Now the jelly jar has fallen over! The water that was in it is dripping onto the floor, and the flowers are going to die! This is a sad part, Mama. It's sad because the first sister has forgotten to take care of the cat for weeks. There's a little layer of sand all over the kitchen floor, and you can see the cat's paw prints in it."

"Beach plum and sedge," Celestine would sometimes whisper, or, alternately, "Roses and lilies." In the dark, small room, she could almost smell it: that odor of disintegration which she had come to associate with passion. Had Paracelsus been right? Did creation really occur through corruption? "But where is the cat?" she would ask.

"That isn't important. What's important is that the first sister doesn't know right from wrong. That's just the way she is. The second sister is different. She's a saint. Even though she'll never get to prove it. And that's what makes her so angry, isn't it, Mama?"

"The second sister is the prettiest one," Celestine would answer, and then she would reach out to touch the soft crown of her daughter's head, to feel the thin line of the part. "So pretty," she would say. But Thule would shake her hand away, impatient.

"Yes, of course she is. You can just see her, standing on top of the highest dune, taking off that white dress with the pink cabbage roses she always wears; she unpins her long braid, and her hair looks like honey when it falls over her shoulders. The next thing you know, she's swimming! Her arms fly up and down. Only we have to remember that she used to be in love. She used to be in love with a boy named Walleroo, but she stopped loving him the day he showed her a chicken neck and said it was his father's peepee. He was a bad boy, Mama, a very bad boy. But even so, she used to love him."

"Love is boring, my sweetheart," Celestine would say. "The second sister learned that the hard way."

"She likes the hard way, Mama. Now all she wants to do is swim. If you were a seagull, you might think that she was a little boat; you might think that her arms were oars. You might think that her lips would taste just like salt; you might think that she is dreaming about nothing at all, or about flying right up out of the waves. She looks strong, doesn't she, swimming so far from shore? The only thing she's wearing is a silver cross on a silver chain around her neck. The water is cool, and she can feel the thick, secret bodies of the fish swimming alongside her. And the truth is, she *is* in love. She's in love with Jesus Christ."

Whenever Thule came to the part of the story about the third sister, she would close her eyes and hope that it would turn out differently. She believed that this part of the story was not subject to revision; she believed that the third sister was most like herself. The third sister was drowning! Why didn't anyone try to save her? But she was too far out, too far away to be seen by the watchful gray eyes of the first sister, her favorite; too small to catch the attention of the second sister, of whom she was afraid. Green above, blackish green around her, the ocean opened into vast hallways where, on her coral throne, Death sat, her gills widening and closing, her gaze cool and impartial. Death was Fortune's sister. "Your sisters have killed you," she said, "and I will tell you why. It is because you have always counted on them for everything. But now you will be my little girl, and I will dress you in flowing gowns of algae. At night you will visit your sisters, and they will finally learn how to weep."

Thule liked to imagine that—the other sisters weeping. Until her mother took in her famous boarder—Johannes Brahms, fat and bearded, his hands customarily stuffed into his trouser pockets—she was a solitary child. Consequently, it gave her pleasure to think about how her absence might stir the hearts of others. But Celestine, as she'd taken to reminding Thule and Max when they complained about the thin and unsatisfying soups she ladled out at suppertime, was having trouble making ends meet. And so, on an autumn day when the wind shuttled through the garden, rattling bracts and pods and dead leaves, Johannes Brahms moved into the set of large rooms at the front end of the apartment.

Thule fell in love with him immediately. She liked to visit him in his library; to sit opposite him in one of his two huge armchairs with flowered covers, and watch him make coffee. Some days he would let her play with his collection of tin soldiers, of which he had boxes and boxes. Other days he would ask her to join him at the piano, and then he would play music so beautiful she could see his fatness peel back and fall away, and, like a needle extracted from a pincushion, a slender young man would emerge—"pure as a diamond, soft as snow," which is how the violinist Joachim described him, years earlier. His sense of humor, characterized as low-German by the biographers, eluded Thule. Once he sat and banged on the keyboard with his fists, explaining that he had done the impossible: written a sonata designed, once and for all, to exorcise the devil housed in the sounding board; as Thule looked around, wide-eyed, to catch a glimpse of the retreating hooves and tail, Brahms burst out laughing. "It does not do to believe everything an old man tells you," he said.

In exchange for his music, Brahms insisted that Thule tell him stories. "Your mother says you, too, have a gift," he'd explained the first time he made such a request. Initially, Thule stuck with the usual—Hansel and Gretel, Big Claus and Little Claus, Rapunzel—but after a while she became more daring. The first time she told Brahms about the four sisters, he inched forward to the edge of his chair, sitting hunched and attentive with his surprisingly long fingers splayed over his knees. He straightened his pince-nez. By now Thule was sixteen years old, and she'd told the story hundreds of times. The sisters had gotten older. Sometimes they lived in cities; the second sister occasionally took to dressing like a man; once, the first sister lived in the far north, married to a goblin whose spirit assumed the shape of a white reindeer. They wrote each other letters. But despite Thule's growing desire to combine them into a single woman, the third sister resisted synthesis, her decomposition into polished bone gradual and horrifying.

Thule suspected her mother would be angry if she knew her daughter was telling Brahms the story; she suspected the story was supposed to be a secret between them. But with the passage of time, Celestine had changed. Her sense of the ironic, which had been leaking out of her over the years, was finally spent; if she thought of the soldier at all—and it's possible she'd given up thinking of him completely—it was with the kind of surprised amusement we reserve for the follies of those younger than ourselves.

In fact, Celestine was turning into an old woman, and, as is the case with some old women, she chose ignorance over wisdom. Her head was now round and wooden, spinning this way and that like the globe in Brahms's library, as she tried positioning her ear to catch the random phrase. She attended Mass with great regularity; little children called her Oma, and she laid sugar cookies in their outstretched hands as if distributing the host.

It's important to remember that Celestine married late in life, and gave birth to her children even later. Now she regarded her daughter's evolving womanhood with something akin to fear; when she came into the bedroom to say goodnight, and to make sure Thule said her prayers, she resisted the girl's attempts to draw her into the story. Whereas with Max, Celestine felt capable of displaying the full range of her talent for motherhood, it was all she could do to bring herself to stoop down and kiss Thule's face, as if, in so doing, she might stir memory into motion and, with it, the flattening winds of erotic possibility.

You see, it was the original ending of the story, as told to her mother by the soldier, that Thule loved the best. She'd only heard it once or twice, years and years ago, and she preferred to keep it silently hidden inside her brain, where she imagined it nestled in folds of gray silk. Later, when she thought about it, she wouldn't know how Brahms had coaxed it out of her. Had he teased her? That was, so often, his method of getting what he wanted.

The fourth sister was the only one with a name, and a life filled with domestic activity. Her name was Clara, and she was married to a brilliant and high-strung man, with whom she had six children. They lived in the same house—still small when viewed from the outside, but unaccountably spacious the minute you entered the door. From its tall, immaculate windows, you could look across the dunes all the way to the sea; had she not been so preoccupied with her love for her family, Clara might have paid closer attention to her other sisters. She was the capable one; she was the one who should have saved the third sister from drowning. But she really didn't have the time. There was the ripped sleeve of Elise's confirmation dress to mend; there were the peonies waiting to be cut and arranged; there was company coming for dinner, and the goose needed basting.

"You're right about that," Brahms said. "She was an excellent cook. But it was in Düsseldorf. The house was in Düsseldorf."

Thule smiled then, and nodded. After all, wasn't this her own technique, her own desire to alter and embroider? "Clara was a happy woman. And the household was a musical one. No matter what time of the day or night a visitor might arrive, there would always be someone, somewhere, making music. But then a bad thing happened. A man arrived, and he was very handsome."

"A young eagle," Brahms muttered, setting a match to one of his long cigars. His fingers shook, and he seemed angry. "A young eagle flying over the alps."

"Perhaps. Everyone in the family fell in love with him. And he fell in love with all of them, too. Only, and this is the mysterious part, there was one of them he loved more than the others. The question is, which one was it?"

At this point Brahms leaned over and pulled open the drawer of a cherry-wood escritoire. Thule could see that it was filled with hundreds of envelopes, tied into packets with blue ribbon. "It was wrong of you to go through my things," Brahms said.

"But I would never do a thing like that," Thule said. She was a little frightened; the old man's eyes had become protuberant and lubricious, as if at any moment they might pop from their sockets like the eyes of certain tiny dogs.

"Never mind," he said. "Go on. You might as well finish."

And so she did: The fourth sister's husband began showing signs of madness. He couldn't sleep; in the mornings, before the sun came up, he would sneak out of the house like a thief, and go down to the beach. He'd never done such things before the arrival of the handsome young visitor. And then one morning, he didn't come back. They all went out to search for him, but there was no sign of him anywhere. The first sister sat, as usual, at the water's edge. "Look in a shell," she said, dreamily. "Look inside a cockle shell." The second sister, her body cupped in the rising palm of a wave, momentarily faced shore. "Pray to Jesus," she shouted. "The blood that pours from his wounds is the blood of all men. Catch it in a basin, and you will know your husband as if for the

first time." The third sister, of course, remained silent. She held
Clara's husband in her long white arms, and sang to him.

"Only that would mean she was one of the Lorelei," Brahms
said. "And I'm sure your teachers have taught you that the Lorelei
live in the Rhine, where they lure men to their death."

"No," Thule insisted. "The third sister didn't lure him to anything. Actually, she didn't know what was happening when she
saw him drifting toward her. His long hair flowed back from his
forehead, and his expression was surprised, just like he'd always
known he'd come to her someday."

"He was mad. He was possessed by demons," Brahms said. "It
was a horrible thing to have to stand by and watch: a man of
genius, a gentle man, who'd spent too much of his time trying to
hear music that would have been better left unheard. Music can
be dangerous. When you listen to music, you can begin thinking
it has its origins in a single source. You can begin thinking God
has a human heart."

"That which is above is one with that which is below," Thule
said softly. "My mother used to say that to me."

"Well, she was wrong," Brahms said. "Listen to me. I know the
truth about what happened. It was the visitor who pushed Clara's
husband into the water. It was the end of February, and it seemed
like the snow had been falling for months. Robert was worse.
When he left the house, around noon, I followed him. I watched
the crazy way he moved through the streets. Sometimes he would
walk right into another person, and then he would back up for
several paces, waving his arms around his ears, the way you do
when you've blundered into a nest of wasps. I loved him more
than I've ever loved any other person in this world. When he
stopped walking, halfway across the bridge, and stood there leaning over the railing, I pushed him into the river. It was the Rhine,
the broad silver Rhine, icing over at the edges. Only, he never
found the third sister. Not then. A man in a boat saved him. He
was freezing cold, and shaking, and it was my punishment to have
to watch him rest in Clara's arms; to have to watch him suck
drops of wine from her fingertips. But he never recovered. A few
months later he died in the sanatorium. Since then, I have grown
heavier and heavier. And one day I'll be too heavy for this earth to
hold me, and then I'll fall through the crust, and the sound I'll

make as I fall will be real music. Do you hear me? Real music! Not this sorry excuse for music, this stuff for which I'm admired."

Thule rose from her chair and came over to where the old man sat; cautiously, because she understood how sorrow abhors consolation, she stood behind him and wrapped her arms around his shoulders. It was getting late; she could hear cymbals releasing their widening circles of sound—her mother was getting out pots and pans, mixing dough for the spaetzle Max claimed looked like maggots. And then, as if it were a latent feature of the room, golden light was everywhere, just for an instant, before the sun fell into its slot, and the city of Vienna darkened.

"But there's more," Thule whispered directly into the old man's ear. "There's a secret. What you don't know is that it was Clara who told him to do it. Clara told him about her sisters, especially the third one. She told him how the third sister knew everything there was to know. She told him how the third sister was shapeless and formless, like the wind blowing off the sea. It was Clara who wanted her husband to fall in love with the third sister."

"That's idiotic," Brahms said. He wrenched his big shoulders from under Thule's thin arms, and went to the piano. "If I don't tell your mama about this, it's only because I know you're still very young and don't know any better."

"I'm not so young," Thule said.

"No?" Brahms sat on the piano bench, and, as he continued to talk, his fingers began moving over the keys, releasing a curl of melody. "Well, perhaps you're not," he said. "Perhaps you're old enough to understand when I tell you that some things are better left alone."

Thule stood by the window, leaning her elbows on the sill. The stars were coming out, a star for each note the old man played. The melody was a sad one: small waves cupped the shore, their undersides a faint and luminous green, the exact color of the third sister's eyes. I'm going to die someday, Thule thought. From downstairs she could hear Max's voice, shrill and excited, and her mama's ponderous response. What would it be like to have ears that couldn't pick up anything but the loudest noise? If only her mama could hear the old man's music, maybe then the cells of her body would quicken, maybe then she would once again be able to listen. "I think," Thule said, "you should tell my mama. I think when she brings you your supper tonight, you should tell her."

But Brahms didn't answer. Though Thule didn't know it at the time, the heaviness to which he'd alluded was already making it difficult for him to lift his hands from the keyboard. He was sinking, then, deeper and deeper into the music; he was beginning to compose the *Vier Ernste Gesange*—the four serious songs—at the first performance of which his admirers would be shocked by the change in his appearance. For even as he acquired greater density, he was shrinking. Celestine would rummage among his clothing while he slept, removing those striped trousers and flannel shirts he wore most often; she would stay up late taking in the seams, hoping to fool him into thinking he was still a big man. His skin turned yellow; his shoulders drooped. In the middle of a conversation, his head would suddenly drop to his chest, and he would start to snore.

And then he received the letter from Joachim, telling him about Clara Schumann's stroke. It was spring, and Brahms was sitting in the garden, his narrow torso sticking up like the tongue of a lily out of the bunched folds of a green lap robe; sunlight glinted off the large silver pin with which it was fastened. Thule heard about the letter as she helped her mother cut up vegetables for soup. Turnips, celeriac, potatoes—Brahms, during the last months of his life, would eat nothing but root vegetables, explaining that only things which grew underground contained the liquids vital to his art.

"No sooner had I handed the poor old man the letter, than he began to shake all over. I thought he was going to fly apart, he was shaking so hard," Celestine said.

"Is she still alive?" Thule asked. "Is Frau Schumann still alive?"

Celestine picked up a little red potato, and scrubbed its skin away with a brush. "He wants to see you," she said. "I don't know. He wants you to help him write a letter. I said I'd be happy to help, but he insisted. You know how he gets. One minute he's as sweet as a lamb, and the next thing you know, he's hurling a book against the wall."

Thule put down her knife and ran from the kitchen. She almost lost her balance on the stairs, grabbing the banister just in time. Still, despite her sense of urgency, she paused for a minute in the vestibule: sunlight filled the small room with color, but she realized that there was no color appropriate to her emotion. Nor did she have a name to give to that emotion. All she knew was that she felt like a lady's long white glove and, at the same time, like the rough arm of a man, shoving into it, ripping it apart.

Brahms sat sleeping in the garden. Insects landed briefly on his wrapped-up body, then took off, buzzing, their wings like gauze. The letter lay open on his lap. Thule could see that it was very short, and she thought about how we're never told enough about the lives of those we love—that all we ever get is similar to the fly's teasing weight on our bare skin, the threads of its legs rubbing together, its purpose beyond our imagining. She tried, delicately, to remove the letter without waking Brahms, but the minute she reached out her hand, his eyelids flew open: his eyes were yellow and dangerous.

"It's your turn now," he said. "Besides, you have a debt to pay. You heard those four songs. Do you think I'm some kind of machine, waiting to turn your nasty ideas into music? I am a very great man, and you are a silly little girl. Your mother, at least, knows what it is like to be human. Why else do you think she turned herself into a stone?"

"Mama said you wanted me to help you write a letter." Thule sat down on a low wooden bench, where the old man's shadow fell across her, making her cold.

"The fourth sister is dying," Brahms said. "Do you understand? It's not just the third sister who dies. And when the fourth sister is dead, then I'll finally be free to look for Robert. Only the interference will continue, of that you may rest assured. The music will be everywhere. It will be impossible to get around it, at least as long as I'm in this body. And afterward—that will be even more horrible. That will be the sustained note of the cello's lowest string, which is the sound your mama's chosen to shut out. But I think the truth is that's the only sound she ever hears."

"I'm sorry," Thule said. "I don't understand why you're so angry at me."

"I'm too old for explanations. Do you have a pen? Your mother tells me your penmanship is excellent. I want this to be perfect. No blots. Nothing scratched out. Tell me if you think you can't do it."

"But I can," Thule said.

The letter Brahms dictated on that afternoon in April never got sent. Word of Clara Schumann's death came before the day was over: a terse message, delivered dispassionately by a young courier—a boy, really—who stood nervously scratching his stomach by the garden gate. Thule, however, watched to see where Brahms hid the letter; she knew that it lay folded at the bottom of the piles of envelopes in the drawer of the escritoire.

And so, rapidly now, the old man's condition worsened. His friends would take him for carriage drives after he could no longer walk, alone, in the Volksgarten. Propped in place against a window, he would sniff up the warm air hungrily; from the basket lunch, he would remove, at most, a dry crust, and pick it to shreds as the carriage rolled past the Danube. But it wasn't long before he ceased to be capable, even, of getting up and down the stairs. He remained in his bed, and requested that Celestine arrange across the counterpane many of his little tin soldiers, suggesting to her the appropriate formations for advance and retreat. Celestine shuddered to think that somewhere, among the many boxes filled with these miniature men, she might happen to remove a soldier whose uniform was dull brown, with a medal shaped like a fish pinned to its chest. She imagined how the little tin mouth would open in a slit. "My darling," it would say, and how horrible it would be, she thought, to realize that even though the voice was no louder than a dropped pin, she'd been able to hear it.

Then, on April third, just as the piano teacher Anton Door was peering, with the bald effrontery of the healthy, at Brahms's head on the pillow, Brahms jerked: his two blue eyes glazed over, and two enormous tears slid down his cheeks. Would it have pleased him to know that his funeral procession filled the streets of Vienna? Mourners came from all over Europe. Thule watched from the front windows of his apartment; she didn't want to follow the six carriages laden with wreathes and flowers to the cemetery; she didn't want to see the coffin being lowered into the ground. Instead—at the precise moment when Pastor Zimmerman was pronouncing his benediction, "Yea, saith the Spirit, that they may rest from their labors; and their works do follow them"—she removed Brahms's letter from its hiding place and took it to the garden, where she knew her mother was sitting in solitary confusion. Then she made her sit still while she read it to her.

" 'Dear Clara,' " Thule yelled, to make sure her mother could hear every word. " 'Here is a little riddle for you. Why did the aging musician grow a beard? Do you know the answer? If you said it was because he wanted to look like God, you're wrong, along with many other people. Also, he didn't grow the beard to make himself appear more masculine, another common misconception. The aging musician grew a beard, my dear one, because he hoped it would muffle the sound of his heart. I am so weak. You would never recognize me. Joachim was here not long ago, and I could see the shock spread across his handsome gypsy face, even though he tried to cover it with his usual charm. I can't hold a pen; that is why this letter is in an unfamiliar hand. It's the work of Celestine's daughter, who reminds me so much of little Julie: the same bony forehead, the same terrible stare. She had nothing of *him* about her, did she? Except the retreat, especially at breakfast, when he poured honey on his bread from that jar shaped like a hive. He could always kill me with a look.

" 'Here I am in Vienna. Every day I watch Celestine carry her yellow basket down the stairs, and I imagine the stairs rising toward me with each descending thump, and I feel my heart breaking under each thump of her big feet. And I think of him.' "

Celestine looked up, surprised. "My feet aren't so big," she said. "Do you think of me as having unusually big feet?"

Thule shook her head. "No, Mama," she said. "But listen. The letter goes on." It made her feel sad to see her mother throw a little wink in her direction—the same wink she'd seen her throw other women as the pork butcher extolled the virtues of a particular sausage. " 'Celestine's daughter,' " Thule read, " 'is pretending that she's only a scribe, taking down every word, but she's devouring what I say. She's falling in love with him, too. She's watching him get up from the table, watching him kiss Julie on her cheek, on the place Celestine informs me is the part of the trout preferred by kings. I think she can feel it, the gloss of honey on his lips, a few crumbs. Maybe she's even figured out that the reason I chose a man's voice to sing the songs of those four serious sisters of hers, is because it is *his* voice. I hope so. I hope so because it's her fault that I've lost him forever. Turned him into music and lost him. I resisted the impulse for so long.' "

"What is he talking about?" Celestine asked. "What four serious sisters?"

"The ones in the story," Thule said. "You know."

"But that was our story," Celestine said. And then she got angry. "It was my story. You didn't have any right to tell him my story."

"Please, Mama," Thule said. "There's just a little more. It's important." She stood, waiting, until Celestine nodded, indicating she should go on. " 'Clara,' " Thule read, " 'stop feeling guilty. Robert's death was an accident. All our lives are accidents. The story of the four sisters has no plot. Frankly, I don't care if you don't know what I'm talking about. There's some gibberish Celestine spouts, some words of a dead pharmacist, I think. Only he got it backward. That which is below is one with that which is below, is how he should have said it. It's as simple as that. There is no God. Unless of course he's hiding in that ridiculous tautology. In which case, it was God who pushed Robert into the river. And you know as well as I that that's a lie.' "

Celestine walked over to a rosebush and snapped off a dead blossom between her thumb and index finger. "You, of all people, should be aware of the fact that I'm deaf as a post," she said. "So it shouldn't surprise you when I tell you I didn't hear a word."

"But you interrupted me," Thule pointed out. "When you interrupted me, you knew what I was saying."

"A lucky guess," Celestine said. Her arms hung at her sides, ending in the white knobs of her fists. "I did everything I could to make his last days comfortable, and this is how he repays me." She sank heavily on the wooden bench, a pale old woman, shapeless, like a manatee. Daintily she lifted her hem above her ankles, and extended one foot into the sunlight. "This is the foot of a princess," she said. "At least, that's how he described it, that night in the cave. Look!" she said, taking off her shoe. "See how slim it is. Can you see how the spaces between the toes are filled with the thinnest webbing? He kissed it. Here. And here."

In the garden, the bees hovered above the roses, from their little particulate bodies came a steady humming sound. The sea was very far away; the soldier had been gone for a long time. On its hinges, the garden gate creaked loudly as, in a Viennese drawing room, three sisters sat drinking tea, while the fourth spread her skirts across the piano bench and began to play. The roses were many shades of red and pink; Celestine looked at each of them in turn, their single notes emerging all at once in a chord, without measure. There was a smile on her face.

She was still smiling when Max threw open the second-story window and leaned out, shouting, *"Mama!"*

"Not now," Thule said, "we have to be quiet now. We have to be very quiet. Shh," Thule said, "Mama's listening."

And so she was. Celestine Truxa sat in her garden listening to the stealthy approach of God.

Ode for Jacqueline

Not Jack, but Jackie
was the member of that 1950's wedding entourage
who mattered to my mother,

Jackie, spoken plainly and in the intimate voice,
who had that *je ne sais quoi*, that *savoir faire*,
that swell sense of style, that wide and lovely face.

So broad it bordered on the beautiful.
And skirting the line became vulnerable,
a face to touch. She—who had instructed

my mother and the women of her class
and generation how to dress,
how to wear their hats, how to carry

their clutch purses and themselves—
was walking up the aisle of a theater
straight toward my mother.

"Oh my God it's Jackie Kennedy," hurried
sotto voce. Though the lady had already
taken someone else's name,

having changed her men by tragic means
rather than plebeian: no futile pleading,
no irreconcilable differences,

and no unpaid alimony, only the nation's
sad and weighty regard. But by 1974, so much
had changed, hadn't it? My mother sat

on one of many wide, blue-carpeted steps
in an overcrowded auditorium.
Suddenly, the air was rustling

with the dove-flutter of sweaty programs,
and my mother could have cried
with joy, or consternation,

but let's say joy. Instead, she squeezed
her daughter's arm, the way
she had always squeezed a child's arm

when the moment of truth or dread arrived
on the movie screen, the same way
she had dug her nails in when the high-wire man slipped—

right over our heads, really—at Ringling Bros.
Barnum and Bailey in 1965 and nearly fell,
but didn't. Jackie O stepping

up the aisle, and my mother and her youngest parked
flat-assed in her path. Sinking in the nails,
my mother pressed to the left,

and Jackie O tightroped past, smiling,
graciously even, as we made way for her.
Jackie, who had that kind of grace.

BARRY GOLDENSOHN

Letter to My Sister

In our father's schoolteacher's hand,
on the margins of recovered snapshots,
nineteen forty-three and forty-four,
the World War murderous still, incinerating
people in cities, alien, remote, unknown,
opposed to us ("And when you've killed
enough they stop fighting," said LeMay),
yet here with Aunt Gert and Uncle Irv
in Williamsport, Pa., American peace
in the family embrace, staring children
propped in front of bleak trees
Thanksgiving, Easter break, and one July,
an apple tree in leaf and in it me
in the branches grinning, dreaming I could fly.
You were two and three, my toy still,
to tickle till you fought for breath,
a miniature person, your suits like an adult's,
fine embroidered shirts and polished shoes.
At seven I wore a tie swung off-center.
In one family portrait celebrating
a leafless road in the Lycoming Valley,
Father looked stern, his arms enclosed
Mother before her nose job and sweet Gert,
in front Renee, a child jewel, me smiling,
dutiful, and you too young for Uncle Irv
to keep in order, staring off, straining
to swallow your fist. And floating on point
above these family groupings, Mother as Giselle
in a long chiffon dress with a ruffled hem.
This was the Home Front. I collected papers
in a red Flyer wagon from the neighbors
for our soldier uncles and the War Effort.
Also here during the war I was chased down

by four older boys yelling "He killed Jesus."
They threw stones but all missed. One boy,
when they caught me, prevented real mischief
by shouting them down that Jesus was a Jew.
In that family world his was the voice I kept,
and because the tribal terrors bred in that old world
were blurred and weakened in this country,
no one here imagined the powers abroad:
gas chambers, firestorms, the jubilant merciless soul.
These loving sisters, husbands, children,
all those adults died in their beds.

Apollo, Aphrodite, and the Poet

*The gods in heavy squabble make the
poet choose which is greater, poetry
or sex*

Choose poetry, you are rewarded with
a winged horse you cannot dismount,
choose sex, you are rewarded with

sexual fulfillment with a mannequin
of Celotex, frigid, stupid, stiff and thin,
choose poetry, you are rewarded with

wings of your own and cannot land,
touch, stop, fall, no arm, no hand,
choose sex, you are rewarded with

heart's enslavement to a prince-
ess, astonished worship, impotence,
choose poetry, you are rewarded with

sexual enslavement to a mannequin
of Celotex, frigid, stupid, stiff and thin,
choose sex, you are rewarded with

sexual enslavement to a horse,
wingéd, that cannot dismount or cease,
choose poetry, you are rewarded with

that choice, the double-pointed knife you knew
you could not grasp, that curse when you
choose poetry you are rewarded with,
choose sex you are rewarded with

Air Drawing

What would be strange
in someone else's bed, familiar
here as the body's jolt
at the edge of sleep—body
persistent, solitary, precarious.

I watch his right hand float
in our bedroom's midnight,
inscribe forms by instinct on the air,
arterial, calligraphic
figures I'm too literal to follow.

I close my book quietly,
leave a woman detective to tough
her own way out of trouble—
local color of Chicago, Sears towers,
bloodied knuckles, corpses.

I turn to him—
who else would I turn to?—
but I can only watch
for a few minutes at a time
the mysterious art of his sleep.

If I touch his hand, he won't know it,
and it's always comforted me
to feel the vibration,
the singular humming in him,
nocturnal humming...

My mystery falls to the floor,
nothing I'll think about tomorrow—
I'm listening for the breath
after this breath,
for each small exhalation...

Is this the way it has to be—
one of us always vigilant,
watching over the unconscious
other, the quick elusory
tracings on the night's space?

That night two years ago
in the hospital, tubes
in his pale right hand,
in his thigh, I asked myself,
Does he love me?

And if he does,
how could he let that steely man
in green scrubs snake his way
nearer to his heart
than I've ever gone?

Walking the Seawall

pacing the ancient earthworks, the fortifications of silence,
I know I am not through with you, I will never be through,
and not one of us who leap from stone

to stone on the road of boulders
that leads to the old lighthouse, not one of us
who clamber the grassy slope

to the lookout point, not one of us
who tread the path along the shore
next to the tangled wall of morning glory,

not one is through or will ever be through
with your ways of hovering, your
ash in the air, your clouds at daybreak

trailing departure, your echoes of rhyme and joke,
hugs of archaic fleece, smiles
a rubble around us, arms

now sunken, irretrievable....
In your unending
absence we keep on keeping

brave and starched.
Beside the point,
a field of muck sinks into itself:

here we scramble on
splintery boards.
Stench of skunk,

stench of animal grief!
You who were here, too, you who waded
in mud beside us,

stand up again in your plaid and freckles
the way you used to once!
Unfurl your striped umbrellas!

Step heavily or lightly, as you did,
twitching and rustling your coats, your furs,
across the bridge from sleep!

Just this single extra
minute
we'll stumble down the uneven beach,

pick our way across the lumps of granite
flung down at water's edge,
creep together just once more

along the jetty at land's end, where
each glittering boulder keeps its fist of stillness
clenched against the wind.

God, He Had a Hat!

Mrs. Rabinowitz is sitting on the beach with her little grandson, who is
   playing in the
sand with a pail and shovel when a great tidal wave suddenly appears
   and sweeps him out to sea.
Mrs. Rabinowitz (shaking her fist at the sky): God, bring him back!
   Bring that little boy right back!
Another tidal wave appears and deposits the grandson on the beach,
   next to Mrs. Rabinowitz.
Mrs. Rabinowitz (after scrutinizing the child for a minute):
   God, he had a hat!

It's the fifties and we stand in the doorway kissing,
suited in the decorum of our age,
shameless in ignorance.

Our betrothal kisses are small, soft,
nervous as rabbits venturing toward the yard
where the mastiff lunges on his chain and the chain

rattles its gravity across concrete.
But my nineteen-year-old
stance is gracious and wifely,

as if bidding an office-bound spouse goodbye,
although I feel the weird prod of your hard-on
poking against gray wool.

Goodbye, goodbye, sweetheart!
Goodbye to your graduate-student face,
your face of a young cynic that blurs as I kiss it!

Goodbye to your innocent almost-pompadour
(soon to be shaved in Basic by the 4th A.D.)!
Goodbye to the startled fur of your brows!

Past midnight, we're through kissing, my father
waits in his fat chair, his haze of smoke,
and you dissolve into the vague hall,

the leafy sidewalks, the lit-up all-night
subways whose overheated cars
rumble into the dark like stage sets.

But now your hat swims back to me,
the one you're wearing in the snapshot
just outside the honeymoon hotel—

gray felt, prematurely middle-aged,
with a brim stiff as cardboard and a crown
that was kind and crushable and soft,

soft as a peach to the touch. . . .

South

They head south, and as they move out from under the dense Baltimore sky toward air and ocean and hot sun, Flo and Matthew beg their mother, Marie-Claude, to tell stories. Flo loves the ones about when Marie-Claude was as young as she is now, and Matthew wants to hear, over and over, how he was born.

Because Marie-Claude does not want her children to talk about their father, who left her at the end of last spring, nearly a year ago now, she gives them the stories they ask for. She tells Flo about Alain Delor, her first crush, and Matthew about the market in Paris where her sac broke as she stood buying peaches in the rain.

But when she begins the story about her first dance, Flo interrupts her. "What about the ghosts in Austria, Mom? Isn't there one about some ghosts at a fancy ball?"

Marie-Claude shakes her head, certain she has never told either child that story.

Using the headrest, Flo pulls herself up closer from the back seat. "Yeah, there is." Some of her mother's fine hair tangles around her fingers, sticky from candy.

"Damn it, Florence. That hurts."

"Maman!" Matthew says, truly shocked to hear an English swearword out of his mother's mouth.

Marie-Claude is surprised, too, and a bit alarmed by the sudden swell of anger. She had promised herself no harsh words to Flo today.

She looks at the enormous clock beside the speedometer: four more hours. She wonders if Flo or even both of them should have gone with their father to New York instead of coming with her to Hatteras. She cannot predict her moods, or the size of Bill and Karen's house, or whether Matthew and Flo will like her friends' children. She wishes she had enough money to fly them home to Lyon for Easter. She takes her eyes from the road to the fields beside them, a movement as welcome as straightening her legs might be. She wishes she could go on looking sideways.

Matthew says, "What story about ghosts in Austria? Watch the road, Maman. What story about ghosts?" She knows he will persist, never forget, not for one day of their vacation.

"It was in a castle," Flo says, "a really old spooky castle that used to be a big deal, like a king or a count used to live there or something. And Daddy was there. I think they were engaged then. Were you engaged to Daddy then? Please tell it, Mom."

Marie-Claude wonders how Flo can know about Austria. Sometimes it feels there is nothing about her life her children cannot uncover, cannot redefine. Once, she had thought there would be a certain amount of grace and mystery in being a parent, and that what went unsaid about her experiences would be respected, and what was revealed would be absorbed without contradiction, occasionally sanctified. Wasn't that how she had treated her own parents' pasts? Perhaps it is because they are American, these children of hers.

"You two tell me stories. I'm tired of talking."

"No," says Flo. "Tell the ghost story. Please, Mommy, please. Please!"

Matthew joins in, and Marie-Claude lets them continue far past the point at which she assumed they'd stop, until their chanting unsettles her more than the idea of telling another story. "Okay," she says. "Okay."

"Your father wasn't with me then," she begins. "I hadn't even met him." She tries but fails to conceal the pleasure she takes in this fact. "I went with my cousin Giselle. She had been invited by her best friend at boarding school in Lausanne, Sigrid. The ball was just outside Linz at a palace that had once belonged to a Habsburg archduke, Franz or Friedle or someone, one of Francis the First's sixteen children. It was later confiscated when the Imperial Family was forced out of the country by the new government. Eventually, it was resold to this Sigrid's grandparents. I didn't know much of the history. I just knew that Giselle traveled with a pack of rich friends and that Sigrid wasn't the only one who could throw a party in her own castle. And I was a bit more like your father then. I loved big houses and beautiful clothes."

"He does not," Flo says, but even in her irritation at one of her mother's jabs, she can't muster up enough conviction to pursue an argument. She has already begun to notice how her father seems more pleased when she plays at Janine's house with the pool than at Lynn's apartment.

Marie-Claude instantly regrets the comparison, regrets this mood on the first day of their trip, and rushes on. "My date was one of Sigrid's cousins, a sullen boy who seemed to want to talk about nothing else but the strategical blunders of the French army. His country gets occupied twice during one war, and he has the nerve to bring up the failure of the Maginot line! But I didn't really care. I was at a ball in fancy dress and could laugh at just about anything."

Flo marvels at the thought of her mother (whom friends call a slob, who always wears her hair yanked back with a brown rubber band off the newspaper) in a ball gown, patiently humoring her date. Flo is beginning to question these images her mother feeds them of her disposition before she married her father. She always makes herself out to have been giggly and lighthearted, the gravity of life never pulling on her until she found herself married with children to raise. But her mother's face is serious, has always been serious, her expression in even the most spontaneous childhood photographs resembling, as her father once said, the portrait of a cabinet minister.

Slowly, the story begins to make Marie-Claude feel better as she describes the carriage they rode in, the view of the Danube, the black horses in the twilight. She senses her children's full attention, Flo's syrupy breath near her ear and Matthew's small body turned sideways toward her, and this audience makes her feel needed in a more extravagant, less basic way than usual.

There is so much to tell: the gardens, the courtyard, the intricate bodice of her dress. Finally, the words she chooses are the right ones; they take on the exact shape and magnificence of the moment they describe. She feels strong and alive, driving her children south on a smooth highway.

She tries not to think beyond it where somewhere there is an unfamiliar dirt road that she must find in the dark. They will arrive late, and Marie-Claude, who promised to be there for dinner, will be treated like a reckless child by Bill and Karen, who are a real family, complete with bicycles and a live-in sitter. And no matter how many games her children invent in the water or how relaxed she feels half-asleep in the sun, the sight of Bill's large, winter-tender feet hobbling down the rocky path to the beach will remind them all each day of what is gone.

"Mom," Flo says, and, when her mother doesn't respond immediately, "Where were the ghosts?"

"The ballroom was enormous and filled with these fabulous gowns and tuxes and champagne goblets. The floor was black marble, and I remember how beautiful my shoes looked against its surface. Have you ever seen black marble? It's so pure and sleek, like sapphires or the fur of a black panther."

"Is that where you saw them, on the dance floor?"

"No, I saw her in the garden." Marie-Claude feels a face, a squat forehead, the sharp edge of an aquiline nose, an ugly, distended mouth, taking shape within her. "She was young, perhaps the same age as I was then, but her face was old with sadness. She held herself straight, upright, but inside she was bent with grief."

"How did you know she was a ghost?"

"When you see a ghost, you know it. You feel it."

"Was she see-through? Did you speak to her?"

"She was different. Something about her movements. And she was so sad, the way she walked around the garden, touching petals and branches, as if she could rid some of her sadness on them. It might have been the way her mouth was shaped. I don't know. It's difficult to describe how I knew."

With a push-off from her mother's headrest, Flo falls back hard in her seat. She pops a sourball from its cellophane wrapper and, after putting it into her mouth, sighs loudly.

A sweet fake-lime smell works its way quickly to the front. "Have I lost you?" Marie-Claude says, finding Flo's bulging cheek in the rearview mirror.

"Nothing happens in this story."

Marie-Claude has an awful impulse (because they are so rude, demanding the story she didn't want to tell, then snubbing it, Flo so impatient, Matthew already asleep) to remind them of sadness. It would be so easy to do. She waits for the resentment to subside, then continues: "She wasn't transparent, but her skin was peculiar. I'm sure that's how I knew she wasn't human."

"What do you mean, peculiar?"

"It was like patina almost, that greenish color that gets on certain metals, you know, the way that bracelet of your father's, the one he wears for his imaginary arthritis, the way that turns when he forgets to make someone polish it. That's how her skin looked up close." Instead of the woman, the wrist appears, its hairless skin beneath the bracelet, the puffed vein that travels from his hand to his elbow. She still loves him. If he does not come back (they are not divorced, not even legally separated), she knows she will never stroke a man's arm again, never tease a man about his hypochondria or infatuation with wealth.

"I like polishing it. He doesn't *make* me."

"Oh, Flo, you don't remember. You used to hate it. The polish stung your eyes. Anyway, that was her skin." Beside her, Matthew's head, which has been slipping and jerking back, slipping and jerking back, finally slides all the way over to the armrest on his door. She checks the lock and feels for a moment what he feels: that delicious surrender to sleep in the passenger seat of someone else's car.

"I didn't hate it. And I still do it, too." Flo thinks of the chance she had to go with her father and his girlfriend, Abigail, to Manhattan instead. She had to choose between ocean and museums, big house with other kids and adjoining hotel rooms (snapped shut at bedtime till morning). All that seems insignificant now. As always when absent, her father has become mild and soothing. She could call him, take a bus back to D.C. He isn't leaving until tomorrow morning. How much could a bus ride cost?

"I did speak to her." Marie-Claude turns around to see if Flo will still listen. Flo doesn't look up from what she is doing: dropping quarters from one hand into another, then back into a pouch. "I asked her if she was enjoying the ball." Marie-Claude laughs. "I didn't know what else to ask!"

"Did you speak French or German?"

"German, I think. But she didn't reply in a voice—it was more like telepathy. But she didn't want to chat. She moved right past me, back to her old route around and around the rose garden."

"This *isn't* the same story."

"I've never told this story to you before, so I don't know what you were expecting."

When she told it to her husband, there were two ghosts. She had wanted him to see what they'd become. She described everything carefully, their movements, their fingers, the shapes of their mouths. *We mustn't become them, Robert, not yet.* But he didn't understand. He had stopped wanting to understand her.

"Mom, you're lying. You always do this."

"What do you mean, I always do this?"

"Change things around. Lie about the truth."

"I'm not lying, Florence." And Marie-Claude sees more clearly the scrolled, unbloomed rosebushes, the small pool, more rosebushes, and the woman traveling through. "I have never lied to you." Each time around the far edge, the woman lifts her skirt so it doesn't catch on a spigot. "I am not the liar in this family."

"Yes, you are. You lie all the time."

"Flo, I do not." For comfort, she knows she can turn to Matthew, who, still asleep, holds a comic book and her sunglasses in his lap. "Name one lie I've ever told you."

"You said we could take Belle with us. You promised we could."

"I thought Bill and Karen would bring their dogs, but they didn't, so I couldn't very well ask to bring ours. We're guests. It wouldn't have been right."

"But you lied. You said one thing and did another."

"Flo, that was completely out of my control. That's not a lie."

"All right, here's a better one," and this is something she's wanted to mention for a while now. "You told me that you and Daddy separated suddenly, that you were both in love all those years when I was little. You always told us that, Mom, that we were born out of love."

Marie-Claude is relieved it's only this, and not some other broken promise. "That's true. It's absolutely true. We loved each other very, very much." There was no day happier in all her life than the day Matthew was born. They were living in Paris then. That morning at the market is still so vivid: the wet stalls, the bag of peaches, the young face of the vendor, the train of pimples across his neck. She was reaching over the cherries to squeeze an avocado when she felt the warmth on her legs, when she finally made the distinction between her own water and the rain. And in the afternoon, Robert brought Flo to the hospital. They climbed right up on the bed with her and Matthew and pretended they didn't understand French when the nurse scolded them. That day was just a culmination of the happiness that had been pooling inside her from the moment she met Robert, yet afterwards there was only more, a peaceful, languorous bliss. They had jokes about it, about how so much happiness was depressing. "All those years, Flo, right up until last year, we were happy. You were born and raised with a tremendous amount of love."

"And then something just happened, just like that?"

"I don't know." Marie-Claude can't bear to play the victim, to actually reveal how bewildered she still is. But her daughter wants the truth. "I just don't know. Whatever happened didn't happen to me." She looks at Flo in the rearview mirror and says softly, with no edge, "Maybe Daddy can explain it better."

"He says it happened slowly. He said it wasn't a big clap of thunder like you say but a wave that gets bigger and bigger until it breaks."

Marie-Claude knows Flo is not making this up to hurt her; she recognizes her husband's similes, stolen from a world entirely alien to him.

"He said he'd been unhappy since before Matthew. He said he hadn't known anything about real love before he met Abigail. He said that when he interrogates witnesses under oath, he always knows when they're lying because—"

"Please, Flo. Please stop."

Marie-Claude slows to the speed limit. Her eyes have been on the road, but she has not been watching. All the windows in the car are open, even hers, which she doesn't remember rolling down. Warm air, much warmer than an hour ago, blows through, and she leans forward to let the wind unstick the shirt from her back. The steering wheel feels loose in her hands, unrelated to guiding the car. And the road, even at fifty-five, is disappearing far too fast beneath them.

She thinks of what she could remind her daughter of. She could tell the story of Flo's last birthday in September, which fell on a weekend she went to her father's alone, without Matthew, and how at first Flo thought he was teasing, not singing at the breakfast table, not alluding to a present hidden somewhere—behind a curtain or in the freezer—and how on the way to check the Saturday mail at his office she expected a surprise party; at lunch she waited for a cake. When he returned her on Sunday, Marie-Claude read the whole story in the raised rash on Flo's neck.

When she feels a bit more in control of the car, Marie-Claude turns to look at the outlet stores beside the highway. She wishes they were driving through France, passing cows spread flat out on a hill. In France they might come across something extraordinary, like a burning barn or a ewe giving birth. Flo might see it first, and, even before she could ask, Marie-Claude would pull over. They would get out of the car noiselessly so as not to disturb Matthew and witness together the hot collapse of a building or the equally overwhelming spectacle of new life dropping onto the grass. They might squeeze each other's fingers in anticipation. But barns in France, she remembers, are made of stone.

From the slice she can see of her mother's face in the mirror, Flo knows she is angry. She decides she will just have Marie-Claude let her off at a bus station before going on to the house. There would be northbound buses every few hours. Her father will be jubilant, even more pleased than if she'd decided on New York from the start.

Her mother is not looking back anymore; Flo has caught her in too many lies. But she is not through. Before she goes, takes a bus her mother will be more than happy to put her on, she wants to catch her in another lie. "You love Matthew more than me," she says. "You do."

This is an accusation Marie-Claude has feared since Matthew was born. She is amazed that this is the first time it has ever been uttered. Until now, she never knew what she would say. Today, the answer slides out effortlessly: "He makes it easier for me, Flo. He's easier to love." She waits for a response, and opportunity to apologize or qualify, but hears only, after a long silence, the crinkling of another candy wrapper. She lets her statement linger between them, hardening into fact. It gives her strength, a sense of utter freedom. They feel like the first honest words she has ever spoken.

More than an hour later, still in the back seat, legs draped over her big duffel that she's already practiced lifting twice to make sure she can carry it to the bus, Flo remembers how she heard the story about the ghost. It was the first night she'd ever spent in her father's apartment, after the separation. Her whole life is now divided into what came before and what came after the separation. This was just after, in those first few weeks whose details are impossible to recall. But she has a flash, in this hot car heading south, of crying in a brand-new bed, begging her father for a story to put her to sleep. He didn't know how to tell a story, he insisted, but Flo did not believe him. *Anyone can tell a story,* she screamed at him. *Anyone.* Finally he sat on the bed and told her how when they were very young, he and Marie-Claude (and Flo remembers this, too, how he said Marie-Claude and not Mom like he used to, as if her mother was now a sister or a friend of the family) had been invited to a castle in Austria. In his version, *he* saw the ghosts. And Marie-Claude didn't believe him. No one did, he told Flo. They all thought he was nuts. But as the night went on, he became friends with these ghosts and, though he couldn't tell Flo exactly how, got them back to their other world safely. Remembering this ending, Flo laughs out loud.

"Look," she hears her mother say softly to herself. The ocean is suddenly beside them. They have reached the beginning of the cape earlier than expected, before dinner, before sunset. Waves crack, then flatten onshore, releasing a sour smell that quickly fills the car. Plump seabirds stand on one leg in the shimmering glaze left behind. Flo forgets to mention the bus station.

Marie-Claude feels Matthew stir beside her. "Look," she whispers again, and he opens his eyes onto the wide shaft of blue alongside the car, turns to her, and asks her to tell him, just once more, the one about how he was born.

Tomahawk

My deaf cousin had a hand in designing the Tomahawk Missile.
The blueprints open on his desk for what was to become
a show-and-tell-style reunion.

I hadn't laid eyes on this exuberant man since chance
threw us together at a party *given by his best friend*
whose brother was your real *father's best friend,*

and whose blind nephew appeared, shook my hand,
and, unprompted, said my name—it was like a blessing.
The deaf men nodded at the blind boy's recognition.

They held me captive, these two deaf friends, and took forever
with frantic mimicry explaining how they knew each other,
firmly guiding the silent dialogue toward the bizarre

intersection of fates: theirs, mine, my father's, my mother's...
The deaf find ways of contacting each other.
They have their own watering holes.

Did he place this decisive warhead above all other
constructions executed during a working life spent
gratefully, perhaps too gratefully, in the government's

employ designing, mainly, destroyers...?
Final proof he was not handicapped by his handicap?
He married a deaf woman, but his two daughters

are normal; I mean not deaf...Both were present
and married. One was pregnant. The other became
more and more present as this Sunday marathon wore on.

Conversation meant—: asking each other questions.
My cousin scribbled answers alongside the next question
on a pad that rustled like a pet hamster in his back pocket.

It was work, talking to that generation's deaf.
It was hard not to raise your voice.
I caught my mother trying to catch my eye

across the smoked fish infested spread
as she mouthed a lipsticky YOU MUST E-NUN-CI-ATE.
Brain-dead from the labor of "catching up"

with veritable strangers with whom I was linked
by blood, I wandered, coffee balanced in saucer,
toward my cousin's study, in vain hope of a tête-à-tête.

He followed, hauled down sheafs from shelves,
while I studied the framed sketches of ship's interiors.
Had deafness helped him achieve these heights of invention?

His face brightened. He strained with strangled voice to answer.
Even I could understand "That's the ticket,"
before he scrawled with Bic on pad. "Deaf...can think better..."

I was about to say "Not all," that I was asking
about him personally, when his daughter intervened
and said, aloud and in sign, that this was "deafism."

He signed: "No, no, not hearing forced me..."
She signed and spoke, indulgent, resigned, admiring:
"So deafness makes you superior?"

I liked the way she stood up to him, and the way he took it.
Trying not to sound like a boorish upstart in a Q&A
disingenuously grilling Oppenheimer, Einstein, or Bohr

with how they felt about their elegant theorems
culminating in so much death, I asked if
he was ambivalent about designing warheads. Question

from left field. Bewilderment squared.
His honked "Wa" was like an inaudible "Come again?"
Forehead painfully wrinkled. Deep-set ridges.

My stomach contracted: Oh God, what have I done?
It wasn't me asking discomfiting questions to hound
this dear, sweet, ebullient man, who had done his best...;

it was my...duty to ask, which appeared to perplex
this...disembodied intelligence...schooled in
focusing on the problem to be solved just as

Husserl bracketed words, [postponed]
this longing to belong to sentences that mimicked
meaningful action, and to block out the politics and social

contexts that could...derail...the (beautiful) concord
between pure thought and necessity. He had the right to think:
Anyone can design a ship, or a missile, that works

like a bigger bullet shot from a bigger gun;
but to invent one that can stop, turn around,
change direction, now that's—invention.

She repeated the question in sign and came back
with: "My father doesn't understand your question."
I spoke more slowly. "You must feel proud at how

the Tomahawk conducted itself during the Desert War."
The praise sent him rocking. So that's what I took so long
to say! He nodded exuberantly in accord.

"Wait. Even though it was for a good cause
doesn't it bother you that the missile
killed many people?" Question from left field.

Flurry of signs between father and daughter.
"My dad says war is horrible but once you're in
it's important to win." "That was true before,

and true as it pertained to the two world wars,
but Southeast Asia . . . was another story."
Groan of dismay. Why should a deaf engineer

be forced to deal with relative ethics, too . . . ? War
made the mental challenge of his work more
challenging, as it did the group holed up at Los Alamos.

The heart sinks when these higher mathematical formulations
become subject to weather, and the stray jackrabbits and *homo sapiens*
"who weren't supposed to be anywhere near the test site. . . ."

This pacific man could not have thought about what the Tomahawk
did to real live—now dead—people.
He was too immersed in the question of how

to get the missile to think, to take into account—the wind.

Anger (Ira)

Our accord's a ruin. One swipe
across the cutting board scatters it.
Away's where I'm going and if that's
blood boiling, leave it on. The heart's
a saucepan, not a cauldron,
the pint-size heart. It can't harm
you unless you've made illicit decisions.
Have you made illicit decisions?
Grit your wisdom teeth and don't expect
to neutralize the dangers with philosophy.
This is not optimum. It doesn't enlarge.
The color is not restored.
Tasteless melons, chatting, vomit—each
has its usefulness, even chickpea soup.
So to stew in our own juices may loosen
our tongues or keep us lively,
but it's more suitable for the very old.
Unlike chicken eggs, it won't noticeably
increase coitus. Unlike coitus,
it won't conserve the species.

Squash (Cucurbite)

Curb your excesses, for I change
and get absorbed too quickly.
See? Already I'm taken in.
Be like water, I told myself, strange
aspiration for a vegetable, but by nature
I was cold and humid. Now
I quench thirst. This makes me
useful, though primarily for the young
in southern regions. Here
in the north, I descend in torrents.
Please, as long as I'm pouring
my heart out, withhold your good opinions.
Your stooped, lanky form is beautiful
to me, but we've agreed to nothing
yet. Consider that I stem—
and stem *from*—longing. Your neutrality
can be preserved with salt water
which frees the body if you add good clay
and bathe in it. Or if you sail.

Sweet Apples (Poma Mala Dulcia)

Their nature? Sanguine, warm and humid
as blood, and they comfort the heart.
Please help yourself. The names I can't
pronounce—something like *paradixani,*
gerosolimitani. Here, have a taste.
I used to be less liberal. I'd cling,
think flesh of my flesh. But where
does that lead? Collapsed brown mouths
the deer won't eat come winter. Better
to harvest while a tree still knows how
blossoming's a way to enter deep into
the world. Even though it leaves you
scatterbrained, a stubble of missed
connections. Or fruitful and worried
by every inching thing. Just look at them—
my sweet, sweet apples. Please eat
your fill. Oh, I expect the nerves will
suffer. But where's the danger that
can't be neutralized? For this, a little
rose-colored sugar is good, a little honey.

Decade

I had only one prayer, but it spread
like lilies, a single flower duplicating
itself over and over until it was rampant,

uncountable. At ten I lay dreaming
in its crushed green blades.

How did I come by it, strange notion
that the hard stems of rage could be broken,
that the lilies were made of words,

my words? Each one I picked
laid a wish to rest. I mean killed it.

The difference between prayer
and a wish is that a wish knows it will be
a failure even as it sets out,

whereas a prayer is still innocent.
Wishing wants prayer to find that out.

Tea Mind

Even as a child I could
induce it at will.
I'd go to where the big rocks

stayed cold in the woods all summer,
and tea mind would come to me

like water over stones, pool to pool,
and in that way I taught myself to think.
Green teas are my favorites, especially

the basket-fired Japanese ones
that smell of baled hay.

Thank you, makers of this tea.
Because of you my mind is still tonight,
transparent, a leaf in air.

Now it rides a subtle current.
Now it can finally disappear.

A Charade

A piece of paper
Which appeared to be blank
But on which we see
Writing had faded.
"My first is of the
Possessive of those
Given to possession.
And my last, the finality
Of that proposition.
In entirety I give
That which in three worlds doth live.
Ungainly in the two;
In all, long-legged beauty,
Much as you."
Upon the paper which had come to fade
We strain to see
An ancient charade.
Can you decipher me?

MOLLY BENDALL

Antonia of Clarity and Seashells

Antonia's midwifed for centuries
turning bloody breeches to
the ripening light. Their heads
wash up to the sun. Light's
trapped here, and the shore's decor

is silky and pink-veined. Trumpets,
periwinkles, cockles, gorgeous mouths
of pain. And babies roll deliciously
on this packed-down beach. Once
she ground her luminescent stones

with herbs—charms for new pain.
It was threatening, the clear glass
and having to hear it and hear it,
until water smoothed the jagged lines.
    —Antonia, pose for me

at your countertop, ready to entertain
in your dinner rings and satin. Babies
swaddled and bedded. The ocean sheen
is never desperate. Aren't you
the singing shell I listen to?

The Subway Platform

And then the gray concrete of the subway platform, that shore
    stripped of all premise of softness
or repose. I stood there, beneath the city's sequential grids
    and frameworks, its wrappings and unwrappings
like a robe sewn with birds that flew into seasons of light,
    a robe of gold
and then a robe of ash.

All around me were briefcases, cell phones, baseball caps,
    folded umbrellas forlorn and still glistening
with rain. Who owned them? Each face possessed a hiddenness.
    DO NOT STEP ACROSS THE YELLOW LINE; the Transit Authority
had painted this onto the platform's edge
    beyond which the rails

gleamed, treacherous, almost maniacal,
    yet somehow full of promise. Glittery, icy, undead.
Sharp as acid eating through a mask. I counted forward
    in my mind to the third rail,
the lethal one, activated, bristling with current
    hissing inside it like a promise or a wish; and the word
forward as if inside it also,

as if there were always a forward, always somewhere else
    to go: station stops, stairways leading up into the dusty
light; turnstiles, and signs indicating this street
    or that. Appointments. Addresses. Numbers and letters
of apartments, and their floors. Where was it, that thing I once felt
    inside me, not immobile, tensed for flight
or capture, streaked with the notion of distance and desire?
    And the people all around me, how many had not

at some time or another curled up in their beds with the shades drawn,
    not knowing how to find the forwardness, or any trace
of joy? Wing of sorrow, wing of grief,
    I could feel it brushing my cheek, gray bird
I lived with, always it was so quiet on its tether.
    Then the train was finally coming, its earthquaky
rumblings building through the tunnel, its focused light

like a small fury. Soon we would get on, would step into
    that body whose headlights obliterate the tunnel's blackness
like chalk scrawling words onto a blackboard.
    I looked down at the hems of the many dresses all around me,
they were so bright! Why hadn't I noticed them before? Reds
    and oranges and blues, geometrical and floral patterns

swirling beneath the browns and grays of raincoats,
    so numerous, so soft; *threshold,* I thought, and *lullaby, disclosure,*
the train growing louder, the feet moving toward the yellow
    line, the hems billowing as the train pulled up,
how they swayed and furrowed and leapt
    as if a seamstress had loosed them like laughter from her hands.

Cerberus

He was the yard dog's yard dog.
His heads accessorized with snakes.
His tail a scorpion's, and his slaver,
a seed bank for Hell's herbarium.
And his bites were worse than his barks.

What did he do in the underworld
except to guard the stairs leading away
from the bitter tide lap of the Styx?
How did he spend his days in the darkness
where only the dead can see?

His rheum-yellow eyes. His chain-mail ears
larger than a basset's. Slower than Charon
at sorting the dead from the living—
yet more accurate, for like the dog
he was, he knew the various scents from the world above:

the grasses and tree bark, scat tracks,
the sweet acrid talc of dried piss. He knew
the dirt-under-the-nail smell of the desperate digging
from the buried-alive, the iron-on-the-tongue
of the licked wound. As ugly as he was,

he had exquisite breeding, a species unto himself.
The stud who would never have a mate. His cock
a huge suppurating rudder stirred the sulfuric
ocean of his realm, a homing device like his anger,
uncircumcised, guiding, probing, a love that could kill.

The Dolphin

When the fin of faithlessness appeared
I watched it circle, dip, and veer
then ride the swells. Where I stood,

on shore among the surf-casters' gear,
RVs and 4 x 4's, I tried to guess
where it would rise, sleek bottlenose

breaking next, so I might measure
the erratic progress that it made
beyond the haunting thought that hung

in me; and so in ten years of marriage
to the sleek warm thigh of that image,
I reached out—my hand pointing toward

the turbulence—and tried holding on
to what revealed itself as only something
passing by. But years are distance

and outside their measurement
is a circumference in which knowledge
circulates, a current of otherness,

vortex and siphon, the place where
the water spout returns to the ocean,
toward which we call out to a wife

or husband who now beyond the safety
of the shore hears that voice
which might turn them from their frenzy.

Safe

He hollowed out the book,
a window in each page,
until he made a safe
to hold the things
that when he touched them
made him tremble:
a stolen turquoise ring,
a condom sealed in foil,
a quarter lid of pot.

His house was safe and warm,
the rooms were bright occasions
and yet his dull knife
scored its way through
paragraphs and sentences
and made a steep-sided quarry
of the book, and made a joke
of the joke about books
and their covers. A need,

like any other, to hide
the self or the things
the self could not contain:
a holy card and rosary,
a boyhood picture
of his father, and a poem
typed on onionskin
and never given to the girl
who never loved him.

The boy who made this reliquary
would like to say what book
it was he carved a square
heart into and made an emptiness
of a world already full:

Flight of the Phoenix?
Voyage of the Kon Tiki?
But he can't remember, except
it was a story of adventure

and nothing like the story
of his life which was filled
with all the threats
and dangers of adventure
without adventure's thrill,
though the thrill is what
he killed when he hollowed out
the book and hid the things
that made him tremble.

Sled

The child on the sled shields her eyes
against the moving glare of snow

looking ahead to where she's been,
growing up impatient for the precipitous

slide of thought into thought.
White fires divide: trees again.

So the landscape is never more
than an exit (the sled veering)

into beauty, not a path to person,
place, the plural surface of touch.

Red paint arrow slashed on pine,
red runners, a reflection, but no

shadow of a wolf stretching, no violin—
just the wing of the arched board, the

child doubling the frozen rope over
her knuckles, kneeling, then lying flat

against the dropping wall of white.
Now the blue digital screen next to our

shared bed bleeds light onto newsprint:
a heap of skulls (the sled airborne), odd

jewels flung on the mind's assessing tray.
I have no way to imagine such numb exactness

but from diminishing height, flung back into
the body on the bed where I have lain awake

all night desiring patience, desiring to read
the skull's pale calligraphy with my fingers.

So late to intercept gravity. Tender gravity,
on that windy hill meant for burial (colliding)

spikes white into cranial fire. Flame-blue
digits pause then drop: no execution, no kiss.

Epith

Here's the little dressmaker
on her knees at your feet,
mouth full of pins:
fixing you in the dummy's image.

Your belled satin shivers like
a goblet of fizzled brut—
You wanted it late in life,
happiness, wanted a little family

but after the kids grew up.
Like a saint on her death pallet,
you longed for an erotic God
but a refined deity—

not some oversexed Zeus
in a see-through raincoat,
spritzing gold coins,
rattling the canopy. No,

at last you've found a groom
born to forget the ring,
the bride's name—
a regular holy ghost.

You forget yourself
with each glittering pin,
each chip off the old rock,
each sip of the long toast

to your famous independence,
negotiated at such cost—
and still refusing to fit.

Rye Harvest

I won't tell you my name. I don't know who you are; maybe you'd pass my name on, and there are many whom I fear now. I would love it if I had nothing to tell you. I have lost nearly everything—country, family, name—but I have retained my honor and gained a story, to my detriment, that I've retold in courts, where I was constantly interrupted and reduced to *yes*'s and *no*'s. I'll give you a more unhalted version than you would have heard in the court.

In the spring of 1991, just before Croatia's Declaration of Independence, the mayor of our village—I'll initial the village as V. (for a generic village), although it didn't start with a V (and wasn't generic, to me at least)—went from house to house to tell us that after Croatia declared its statehood, the Yugoslav People's Army and Serb Chetniks would try to drive all the Croats out of the region to create a pure Serbian Republic of Krajina. "What guns are you comfortable with?" the mayor asked. "What did you do in the Yugoslav People's Army?"

I didn't believe him. I expected him to be locked up by the Yugoslav police any moment. I looked toward the door and was surprised that it was all quiet out there, except for a pair of cats fighting or making love.

"Infantry? Artillery?" He leaned over me, and I could see the hairs in his nostrils and atop his nose bulb, like sparse grasses on a shiny rock. This man had stolen my two goats that I'd let roam free in the grassy ditch in front of my house. They'd disappeared, and a month later I recognized them tied to the lamppost in front of his house. He probably made cheese out of my goats' milk. He smelled like chevre even now. Anyway, I had gotten over the losses, and I answered, "I worked in radio communication. I did spend three months in training, and I can handle a basic rifle."

"Oh, good. Others can handle guns. You'll be in charge of the radio tower."

Soon I spent nights in the postal relay tower on a hill above the village, typing Morse code, jerky alterations of long and short beeps, and talking on the radio. I developed a network of people to chat with—radio communicators from Croatia, Serbia, Bosnia—and to trade in plum brandy, CDs, produce, medicinal plants, mushrooms (I collected them in the woods). Sometimes I picked up warnings when Serb jets were about to fly over our area to bomb. Then I'd call the priest by phone, and he'd toll the church bells and burn incense as though to hurt the devil's eyes, and sometimes he'd burn up so much incense that it smelled as though the village was burning. People hid in the basements, but some didn't bother. Jets flew over us on the way to factory towns, to demolish the factories and terrorize townspeople so they'd run away. Once, before dawn, when I was already home, sleeping with my cat, the jets bombed—burned down the mayor's barn, struck the tower foundation. The electricity went out. Next day we brought in new cables, and were back in business, but a hole gaped in the base of the tower so that it looked like an old rotten and branchless oak that had grown a couple of huge mushrooms on top.

Everybody was more alert than usual—dreading what was to come, suspecting, being suspected, yet energized to work, talk. There was a solidarity among us; we would defend what was ours. I talked even with the mayor, about the habits of the red fox, what mushrooms you couldn't eat while drinking brandy, and so on. I cooked my favorite mushrooms for him and his wife, and when he went out to get blood sausages to go with that, without any thought, his wife and I embraced and made love, standing, next to the stove, and we continued on the sly, in haystacks, at least once a week. There was something erotic about the fear in which we all lived, and an incredible amount of spontaneous screwing went on. I won't get into all that, other than to say that I actually enjoyed myself, for a while. I was now twenty-five, felt clever, expanding my horizons beyond my village through the radio— I just didn't know how far these horizons would stretch me.

Now across from us over a river valley sat a Serbian village, and on the other side over another valley a Croatian village, and in the distance you could see blue Bosnian mountains, from where Yugoslav troops—supposedly neutral but fighting for the Serb side—fired projectiles into the Croatian villages. Ours was mixed ethnically and thanks to that rarely bombed. I had never worried about ethnicity, but now we were forced to think in those terms, and I still didn't bother to, much. In the village of about two hundred, I'd say there were eighty Croats, seventy Serbs, some Hungarians, Czechs, and Italians. Before World War II, half the village was German and Italian, but only one German remained. The partisans left this one German because they'd eaten the bread he'd baked. The bread was so good that the captain said, "You got to stay here and keep baking that bread of yours for the rest of your life!" And the old stooping German did just that, with his large cracked hands, cracked from the heat of crusts and yeast.

Once Serbs encircled us, I felt strongly that I was a Croat. I was proud of it, felt offended by the aggression and all that. Now, I'm neither proud nor ashamed of it. The identity is certainly useless to me. I get nothing from it, and I have nothing to give it. If you come from some wonderful country like France or Italy, you gain immediate prestige with an aura of culture, but if you come from some godforsaken place like Croatia or Slavic Macedonia or Latvia, what do you get? Nothing, except to be categorized as an alien, a collaborator. Abroad, I'd be inclined to be ashamed of being a Croat if I didn't see that this system of grading ethnic identities wasn't a bunch of chauvinist crap even if under the guise of anti-chauvinism, such as, for example, to say that all Croats, Azeris, Armenians, and so on are hotheaded chauvinists who don't deserve respect, unlike the wonderfully cosmopolitan and tranquil Swedes and the Dutch. Anyhow, I cleaned my rifle every night to make sure it would fire smoothly at the invading Serbs. Still, although I hated the Serb armies, I didn't hate the Serbs around me.

My best childhood friends were all Serbs. I had grown up alone with my grandmother and spent most of my time with my friends; my father had left for Sweden in the first wave of worker migrations, and we never heard from him again. There were rumors—that he'd been killed by the Yugoslav secret police, that he'd married an old billionaire, that he was a drug lord. My mother left for Germany and cleaned office buildings there; she came home for a month every Christmas, but after she remarried, I saw her only two or three times. Now and then she'd send my grandmother a check, to cover school supplies for me. Since I grew up without a family, friendships became extra important.

Even later, when I went to Germany for a couple of years as a Gastarbeiter, with my Serb friends I hung around and drank my daily beer and played soccer on Sundays. When the war started, we were all back in the village, and sometimes two of them, Jovo and Dragan, visited me in the tower to play cards. They were part of our village army, along with most other male Serbs who were drafted. Only a few—those who probably were Serb nationalists or who felt threatened in Croatia—drove off to Bosnia and Serbia right before the war, and most who stayed with us sat at night at the edge of the village, trying to figure out how we could actually defend our fields and homes.

We were not an organized army. It was hard to know who was in charge of us. If we simply banded to defend the village, that made sense, but to be part of the army with an unclear chain of command made me uncomfortable. We called ourselves the Croatian army—at the time Croatia wasn't recognized and wasn't a country but a region of chaos—simply because on the other side was the Serbian army.

Pretty soon it became clear that the special police controlled us, and it wasn't always clear who controlled them—whether it was Mr. Marcup, a businessman, or Tudjman's party (Croatian Democratic Union). Often it seemed nobody controlled them because they had a free hand in many ways, especially with the women. Half the Croats in the police group came from other regions—except for a couple locals—and spoke mountain dialects. The other half spoke some kind of nasal English. They came from the States, Canada, Australia, Argentina—hard-core types with tattoos; there was a wild energy about them, like around a band of strays who are suddenly intoxicated with their ability to inspire fear.

I found it disturbing that the special police often searched Serb homes—even the homes of my friends—for guns, and sifted through their papers. Now I know this was a standard intimidation strategy, essential to ethnic cleansing; Serbian police did the same in the villages under their control.

As soon as the police got to the village, they usually came to the radio tower and wanted me to make them coffee. They smoked and looked out from the observation tower with powerful binoculars. I got to know the commander, Goran D., with a blond crew cut in the manner of the American marines, and his assistant, Igor M., whom I knew from my high-school days—he used to play soccer for our school, and was a particularly brutal defense player, taking pride in his slide-stop. Igor had a lisp since he had no front teeth, probably lost them in soccer. His back teeth were perfectly healthy and white. While he talked, I was distracted by the lolling and bobbing of his tongue.

"Hey, what do you think?" the commander, Goran, asked me once, after we'd exchanged a couple of jokes and slapped each other on the shoulder. "Are those Serbs of yours trustworthy?"

"Yes, why wouldn't they be?" I was no longer laughing. "I've known them since childhood, they've never cheated me. We slaughter our pigs together, and together we harvest and dance barefoot every fall on our grapes in the barrels to squeeze the juice out and make wine; we even cut down the oaks and cook the planks to curve them for these barrels. We are all just peasants, not nations."

"Oh! You talk slippery, more like a city slick than a peasant. Why do you say Croats, too, like we'd take anything from anybody that wasn't ours?"

"What I mean is, our fellow Serbs wouldn't want any army to come here and burn down their houses."

"Any army," he echoed me sardonically.

Talking to the policemen, you had to be on edge—they drove their points brutally. But mostly they joked obscenely (in their rounds, they collected jokes); strange, now I can't remember anything funny. They offered me brandy—and gave me bottles of Jack Daniels to keep, which I did—although as a rule they didn't drink themselves. I had a sip now and then, knowing that wasn't smart. They even offered me women if I cooperated with them and helped them monitor the local Serbs.

But two weeks after our "cooperation" started, they shouted at me that I hadn't collected any information, that I better shape up, what use was I as a communications director, and so on.

One late afternoon, as I was harvesting rye in a lush green and orange splendor of late summer fields on the edge of deciduous woods, I heard screams. I went over the hill and saw two men handcuffed to two young oaks. Several members of the special police force were punching Jovo and Dragan, and kicking them with their boots.

I laid aside my sickle, and rushed over.

"What are you doing?" I shouted to Goran.

"What do you mean, what are we doing? Isn't it obvious? Just minding our business. Ask what they are doing."

"What?"

"They want to run over there, join their Serbian brothers."

"How do you know?"

"We know."

"For sure?"

"Somebody overheard them in a tavern."

"So it's just a rumor. I don't believe they'd do it. Why don't you let them go?"

"How come you trust Serbs?"

"These guys are my friends."

"Your friends. Well, they aren't friends of the Croatian people."

I insisted that they be freed, but Goran laughed. "I don't have the keys to their handcuffs."

"Who has the keys?"

"The guy with the keys is gone to the grocery store."

"At least you can stop beating them!"

"All right, we'll do that. But let this be clear to you." He leaned his face into mine and pushed his forefinger into my neck, into the V of my larynx, so that I couldn't swallow my saliva. "If they go over to the other side, we'll be back, and we'll continue the beating where we left off—but this time it'll be on you. You understand that? You still vouch for them?"

"Of course I do."

"What's 'of course' about it? Make sure the 'course' doesn't get you. You must know about them, haven't you done your homework?"

And the policemen began to walk off toward a jeep.

"Hey, who'll unlock them?"

"What's wrong?" lisped Igor. "They look good like this."

And the police drove off.

The two friends groaned. Jovan thanked me; Dragan kept moaning, hanging from his handcuffs.

I went home to get a metal saw and brandy to wash their wounds and to soothe their throats, but when I got there, the police were back, and this time they had the keys.

Naturally, after the treatment they had suffered, my two friends ran away. I don't know where they went, but where would they go? Who knows, maybe they just fled abroad.

The police came three days later, and Igor asked me, "So where did those friends of yours go?"

I was surprised that he now could shape all the consonants while he used to loll his tongue to fake most of them.

"How would I know?" I shrugged.

"How wouldn't you know? You were so chummy with them, they'd confide in you, wouldn't they? And if they wouldn't, why did you put your neck on the line?" He grinned widely. He used to cover up his mouth, embarrassed by his missing teeth, but now he had fine porcelain teeth. Such teeth you couldn't get in socialist dentistry before; this was private enterprise, expensive stuff.

"I didn't even know they had disappeared." I didn't want to appear nervous, but I spoke out of breath anyway.

"You guaranteed that they would stay with us."

"No, I said they wouldn't run over to the Serb side. Anyway, I'm not their keeper. I couldn't lock them up. They are free to go wherever they like, why not?"

"Deserters. They didn't stay with us. Where do you expect their loyalties to lie anyhow?"

The cops kept repeating their line, and it would have been a boring conversation if there hadn't been a distinct sensation of threat to it. They told me to walk out with them to the back of the building, gave me a glass of wine. "You never know," said Igor, "this may be your last. No point in leaving without one. Besides, you might enjoy it better if you're a bit tipsy." The commander, Goran, didn't say anything. He used a nail clipper, and in a moment of silence, the clips sounded loud. When he'd done clipping his fingernails, he took off his boots, sat on a thick root, and clipped his toenails, and then with his fingers cleaned the dirt between his toes.

The police thugs formed a circle around me, and they took turns hitting me. Fists, boots, gun barrels, clubs. A blow brought me to the ground. I had a sensation of heat flashing through my brain and down my spine. I passed out, and when I came to my senses, it was getting dark, a blue evening. An old man with a sponge of cold water was washing my head. He told me that I'd been out for an hour. "Can you walk?" he asked.

No, I couldn't walk. The man helped me to his tractor and drove me home. My mouth hurt and bled. I was missing most of my front teeth. My right flank was soaked in hot blood, and I shivered although it wasn't cold.

"Why are you helping me?" I asked the man, and recognized him as the old baker. "I hope you didn't ask them to stop beating me?"

"No, just watched from the side."

"Did they see you?"

"Sure."

"Do they know you are helping me?"

"They know everything. What do you want? That I dump you in the field?"

"Might as well."

He drove me to my grandmother's place and gave me a loaf of soft bread, but I couldn't chew it; it would mix with the blood of my gums. For now I wasn't hungry; I was drinking my own blood with each swallow. My tongue got stuck against my palates, and I could hardly unglue it.

My grandmother nursed me for days. She was, as I said, my only relative in the village. So that makes it understandable why I stuck by my friends so stubbornly, though, obviously, it did me no good. Grandmother washed my wounds with brandy and garlic juice and laid slices of onions over them; she gave me a lot of goat milk to drink. The more time passed, the more I hurt. As soon as I made a step, there'd be a painful jolt in my head. I wondered whether I had internal bleeding. I knew I couldn't take any aspirin, because it would increase the bleeding. I couldn't breathe in hard; my side scorched, where the bayonet wound, or a knife wound, was healing without stitches. It needed stitches, and my brain a CAT scan for the concussion. I'd read you could die from blows to the head even a week after you got them, and I thought maybe I would die soon. How would I go to the hospital now? If I went into the town, I'd pass checkpoints. How could I tell them that the Croatian police beat me? I could lie, but the police probably knew about me.

I had fevers; my wounds were probably infected. But I was at peace. Nothing to be done. I could die, for why live? Death would be easy in the moments when I was passing out anyhow.

My grandmother called up my uncle Ivan. The phones still worked. He drove over from the town of K., packed me in the trunk of his Opel, and drove me to Zagreb. During the ride, each stone on the road jolted my brain.

On my Yugoslav passport I went to Hungary by train. The border was still controlled by Yugoslav police and the Federal Army. A tired cop asked where I was going. I said, "To the hospital."

"Don't you have hospitals in Zagreb?"

"I couldn't go to one in Zagreb. Their military police beat me."

"Would the hospital people know that? Anyway, why should I care? Keep going."

Clearly I couldn't be used as a soldier by any army anymore. Who'd want to keep me?

I tracked down my mother in Mannheim, Germany, and she said she'd let me stay with her for several months, or, as she put it, "until you get your feet on the ground" (or cement). Divorced, she lived with a parakeet, who kept squeaking at the most ungodly hours. The cage was right above my bed next to the window so the bird could enjoy sunlight—and it was sunny about ten minutes a week, from what I could tell. For the cage floor, she used newspapers, mostly the porous kind, like *Die Zeit*. So at night, crap would melt holes in the paper, and this mush of cellulose, lead, piss, and crap dripped on me. I moved the cage to the other end of the room, but my mother put it right back above me. So I bought the thickest glossy magazine I could find, *Der Spiegel*, not to read but to fortify the cage. When I opened the cage to place the magazine inside, the colorful shooter flew out. Only now, as the bird kept flying, did I notice that a window was opened, just a crack, but the bird flew right out. My mother was furious, and she wept, and then threw me out. So much for family.

Luckily, I had already made friends with a student of theology in Heidelberg, where I hoped I could study radio communications technology. Hans let me stay with him for several weeks.

I applied for asylum status in Bonn. The judge, who listened to half of my story, turned me down and said, "We've recognized Croatia as an independent country. One of the conditions for the recognition was that human rights be fully respected. The Croatian foreign minister vouches that all refugees will be safe upon return. You as an ethnic Croat have nothing to fear."

"To begin with," I said in German, "the local commander of the special police force became a member of the parliament. His assistant, Igor, became the chief of the police in the town that's the county seat for my village. The only way for me to live in Croatia is to get the papers in that police station that controls my county. How would he react when he saw I was back? I'd rather not find out. He probably thought they had left me dead in the field. I know there is a legal system there that looks good on paper, and if I knew people of influence and had enough money, I could sue everybody who beat me, and he knows that. This chief of police would want to eliminate me."

The clean-shaven judge with golden glasses nodded and said that whatever I was saying was psychological and personal, not political. "If everybody sought revenge or the means to prevent revenge, then most of the region, up to twenty million people, could seek asylum, probably in Germany. Wouldn't that be absurd? Since you aren't a political enemy of the ruling party— and the ruling party even allowed opposition to participate in elections—and you made the point that you were apolitical, belonging to no party, I deem that it would be safe for you to return to Croatia." He gave me one week to leave Germany for Croatia. When I asked for my passport, he said they would mail it to Zagreb and would issue me exit papers that would allow me to travel only to Croatia.

Naturally, I didn't go to Croatia. I tried to get asylum papers at the U.S. Embassy in Bonn. When the officer found out that Germany had declined my application, she discouraged me from applying, saying that the Germans were much better informed about the situation in the Balkans than the Americans.

Hans wondered how he could help me. He suggested that he could find me a novice position in the Benedictine monastery in

Ziegelhausen, just north of Heidelberg. "You'd love it there," he said. "You could walk on the Philosophenweg in the woods every day, brew beer with them, and I don't think that they would even need to report you to the state. Anyway, their giving you a shelter would make you immune, I'm sure."

Monasteries never appealed to me. Besides, I believed in America. When all else fails, go to America—hasn't that been the European formula for the last three centuries?

As we talked, I stared at Hans. With his closely-cut black hair, a wide nose, and a big jaw, he resembled me.

"Why don't you lend me your passport!" Before I was even aware that I'd formed the thought, I'd shouted it. "Get a visa at the U.S. Consulate, and lend me your passport."

"What do you mean, lend?"

"I'll mail it back to you from the States once I get there."

In a week, he gave me his passport with a tourist visa stamp that was valid for one year.

In the States, with the help of the passport, I got a driver's license, and the license is everything, your citizenship, practically, or so it seemed. It didn't bother me that I didn't have a green card. There were many illegal aliens in the country, and now and then there was an amnesty program.

But pretty soon it began to bother me that since I had an accent, I had to identify myself, by nationality, when I worked as a porter at a Hilton. If I said I was an American, people raised their eyebrows.

"This is a nation of immigrants," I said, "isn't it?"

"Sure, in a way," they'd say, "but where do you really come from?"

So I'd have to say I came from Germany, and sometimes, when Germans cheered up at that thought and switched to German, I had to decline to speak in German—they would have read me— and a couple of times I claimed I was a Romanian German, a Volksdeutscher. I found that uncomfortable, especially when a German journalist visited me to make a report on how Volksdeutscher lived in the States. I declined the interview. Lying itself wouldn't bother me so much, but somehow the sensation that I could never introduce myself did. I felt my old land—I don't mean Croatia, but my region and village—to be part of me, and never to mention it hurt.

I began to introduce myself by my real name and real region. I legally changed my name from the assumed German one to the Croatian one, although that seemed odd: if you have a foreign-sounding name, you change it to something like George Johnson, not something even more foreign. On my state tax return—I wanted to become an honest American—I filled out the name-change forms.

A very simple thing, however, happened. After a year, when the visa on the German passport expired, the INS officials showed up at my address, at my uncle's. They tracked me down through my employers.

The officers, when I opened the door, asked, "Are you Hans K...."

I said that I wasn't the German, but while I talked to them, for some reason, I had a strong German accent.

They showed me Hans's photo from the visa application, the duplicate, and said, "Sure looks like you." I said that was just a coincidence, which of course it was, but they shackled me. I asked them to release me so I could show them my papers—new driver's license, income forms, and the tax returns, where they read that I had changed my name. I'd forgotten it was all there. I told them then the whole story—they were even touched—and when I asked to be allowed to appeal to the courts, they agreed, and let me go free so I could pursue the asylum application, and gave me three months to do so, and they gave me extensions, so a year later the deportation trial took place.

There's one system of justice—with jury—for the citizens, and another for the asylum seekers, without jury. For the latter, a judge and a lawyer suffice.

The judge listened to the INS official demanding that I be deported and to my lawyer—a Jewish woman of Polish origin who had just graduated from the University of Chicago law school and who volunteered to protect me—that I be allowed to stay. I trusted my lawyer's sharp mind. I was attracted to her, but the asylum was more urgent, and I was as timid as a schoolboy around her. She told me that if I married an American, I'd easily become a legal resident, but uncertain of how to introduce myself, I hadn't talked enough to any women to develop a relationship.

I was the only witness for myself. The judge asked me many questions which worked more as an interruption to my story than any kind of clarification. Whenever I managed to start explaining what had actually happened, what kind of secret police Croatia had, he'd ask me something technical and irrelevant, like the name of a river.

During the testimony, the judge nodded off while my lawyer questioned me about the threats that awaited me at home (the Croatian army's offensive that drove Serbs out of the region paved the way for ruthless police rule in the provinces). When it was His Honor's turn again, he woke up and said, "Now, in your testimony, you said that your grandmother had to leave your village before the Croatian forces attacked, peacefully, and in your written statement in the application for asylum you claimed that your grandmother was kicked and knocked down and forcefully taken out? Can you explain the discrepancy?"

"Yes, I can. My English wasn't good enough when I submitted the application first, and my uncle, who was writing this, misunderstood me, and we never got to correct this."

"Why would the Croatian army drive her, as a Croat, out?"

"It was a blitz attack. They first drove everybody out—they had no time to check IDs and all that—so they could bomb the hell out of the place without worrying about the civilians."

"Why wouldn't you want to return to your village?" asked the judge.

"I would, Your Honor, but the village doesn't exist. It was razed to the ground from what I have heard."

"What army did that?"

"It's hard to tell. After I left, Serbs bombed and took the village, and the village changed hands several times. The war activity destroyed it."

"So where would you live if you went back?"

"So I'd have to live in Zagreb at first, and to my mind, that's the same thing as living in Chicago—I could just as well live in Chicago or Los Angeles."

"Well, why not go to Zagreb?"

"One of the policemen is now a big shot in Zagreb." I even

added that the village mayor would be after me because he'd found out that I'd had an affair with his wife.

At that, the judge threw up his arms. "There's no such thing as asylum for protection from jealous husbands. Moreover, to the question of whether you were a habitual fornicator, you answered negatively on the application form. So what can we believe of you?"

"It wasn't a habit. And, I haven't had sex in two years."

The judge glossed over my final reason for the asylum application: namely, that since the war in the former Yugoslavia would probably keep going on for a thousand years—if you believed the American newspapers, you'd have to believe that—I could not live there with my post-traumatic stress syndrome.

He replied: "This country has invested enormous resources to make sure that the peace in the Balkans would take hold, and therefore I see no reason why the country should put even further resources in taking care of refugees who would apparently be safe in their native regions."

The judge asked for the proceeding to be adjourned. When he came back, he asked me: "If your application is denied here, what other country would you consider moving to in order to apply for an asylum?"

My lawyer asked for clarification: "To apply to stay here or in that country?"

I thought for several minutes—I was dazed. What, will they deport me? Are there cops around? I looked over my shoulder. Cops, no matter what nationality, terrified me.

The judge asked again, and my lawyer urged me to answer.

"Australia," I said. I knew nothing of Australia, except that it was something like Texas stuck in the middle of the ocean.

The judge then read the verdict, off the top of his head, from what I could tell—something like this:

"Since the claimant was not wounded severely enough to seek hospitalization, there is no ground to suspect that his life would be threatened in Croatia. If the group of men from the police force had wanted to kill him, they could have done so in the war. Now in peace, the likelihood that they would have motivation to kill him is low, according to my estimate.

"The claimant has one month to leave this country voluntarily for Croatia at his expense or to Australia if the Australian government agrees to accept him. If he doesn't leave in thirty days, he will be deported to Australia within ninety days or to some other country that agrees to accept him, and if none does, he will be deported to Croatia. I will give him five years before he may reapply for asylum in this country."

And that was that. My scars, my passing out, my bayonet wound, the teeth knocked out, that didn't qualify as a credible threat and something that should have gotten medical attention.

I know that many people who had never been threatened or were threatened much less than I had been—Croats from Serbia and Serbs from Croatia—got the asylum.

I marveled that the judge, who probably lived in wealthy suburbs—played golf and retold stories from the court to entertain people at cocktail parties—that he should judge who was safe and who wasn't in the Balkans. Anything that deviated from the formula—divisions along the ethnic lines—didn't work for him and for the German judges.

So what do I do? Go retell my story in Australia? Why would it work there? They'd say the Germans and the Americans know better, and if they think you'd be safe, why should we think otherwise? Could I end up like that man without papers who lives in a Parisian airport? No country, no papers, only a story about no country and no papers. That's why I am writing this down, so I can have more papers (an uninterrupted story) to simply hand over to whoever wants to judge my applications.

I thought all this would sound more dramatic. If you say something that is not true often enough, you convince yourself that it is true; and if you repeat something that is true often enough, you begin to doubt it. So here I am, a confirmed un-amnestiable illegal alien. Still, I admired the fact that after the judgment, I was free to walk away from the court. I had thought I would be handcuffed and deported on the spot. That they left it up to me to come back to be deported—that almost convinces me that I would indeed like to stay here.

I am not saying that I'm not going to Australia or Finland (Finland, Endland?). If I leave the States, I want at least my story, such as it is, to stay. I think many Americans might want to know that there's no jury for foreigners, asylum applicants, here. And they should have the opportunity to know that the Balkan problems can't be reduced to a chemical formula of adrenal hatred among different ethnic groups. Am I asking to give a geography lesson? Should I include a map here, or somewhere, of my old land? Better not. For me, that land is disappearing into unreliable memories, and I can't say that I regret that.

Unspeakable

When Gus sees his father,
they don't speak of it.
His mother is dead.
What was it that he did
when he was ten?
He remembers his father
stripping him and hosing
him down outside,
and beating him
with a peeled switch.
Sent to his room without dinner,
he grew up dreading
the evening meal. And yet
he bought his father's
little store of stoves
and he features sets
of cooking pots.
He has every utensil necessary
and fixes himself elegant food
but then, if you are his guest,
he serves very small portions
and hustles it away saying,
"Oh, you should see the dessert."
He advertises over the local radio;
his stove shop, cast-iron stoves,
the warmth of home, the real home
where you can draw near
touching one another's feet and hands;
leaning back in your chairs,
everywhere familiar,
creating your own past.

A Visit

What she is waiting for never arrives
or arrives so slowly she can't see it:
    like the river
    bluing silver

and wearing minutely deeper into its channel,
the flow hardens to carved stone as she fidgets
    beneath the whirling fan
    impatient for the train

that rocks us above the water to arrive:
Her sisters and brothers gone, she ventures alone
    through sunlight
    and moonlight

weaving shadowy faces across the peeling walls...
—Speeding toward her, is it you and me she spies
    in the trembling train
    windows while the engine

hauls us down rails that swerve under wheels
rolling through her brain? Faces burn
    through dirty glass,
    smears of lips and eyes

dissolve to spots of darkness swarming between
her eyes so that swaying apartment towers
    crumble as her nostrils
    prickle from the landfill's

ammonia that hangs above the stacked, crushed cars.
The rails that take us to her pass boxcar after boxcar
   like the successive selves we are
   as she dreams us coming closer,

switching track to track: Now the super unbolts
her door as she calls: "Oh is it really you?"
   —the wheels rolling
   through her head bringing

us face to face with raveled bandages, crutches
leaned in dusty corners, terraced mountains of
   yellowing newspaper.
   Framed above her chair

a picture of a prairie sprawls round a covered wagon
and the horse she rode as a girl, her eyes
   fading points of light...
   Again she calls out

above the train's approaching rumble: "Is it you at last?
My eyes have got so bad people's faces
   are all blurry... Now
   tell me, it is *really* you?"

But already the rails are switching, bearing
our waving hands away at the speed of thought
   over the stony waters that
   ceaselessly pour out.

CHANA BLOCH

The Collector

1

The Roxie is down the street from the locked ward
where I left my husband.
I took the children to the movies that night,
a comedy about the war:
in the candy dark, the laughs
went off like explosions. Here's the letter he left me,
a green crayon scrawl. These
are the sayings I tacked to the wall
and the meager patience
I lace myself into. Here's the Primo Levi I carry
in my pocket: only catastrophe
will calm me. And here's
the comfortable voice of my so-called friend:
You had it too good.

2

Unshaven, in pajamas at noon,
he surveys yesterday's leavings:
dirty socks on the sofa, the unflushed toilet.
Yes. He's home again.

The *shlup-shlup* of his slippers
down the hall to the kitchen
where he rules by gag law: *Don't say that.*
I'm a sick man. It's not my fault.

I shake the dry pod of my heart
and pray for a twitch of feeling,
a little rattle of love.

His fist pounding my shoulder
demands absolution.
I'm allowed two sentences: *You're fine.*
You're going to be fine.

3
I have always saved
what I couldn't understand. I collect
what he does the way other people
save string. Bottle tops, trivets, bone buttons
with tag-ends of thread in them, gritty
loose change—
                 I don't know how to sort or let go
so I stash it all, rusted feelings
without handles or wheels.

And the brain with its gullet, its gut,
its gripping, its kneading, its
squeezing-of-the-damp-out all day and all night—

I have kept everything.

No Orpheus

*When he sang of what had passed, the trees
would lean toward him, he could suspend the
suffering of the damned, he could bring back
the dead.*

Don't look back!...

Hell is a spotless room
overlooking the ocean; she

wants out.

"I'm heading for nowhere, what do I have
to look forward to?"

She used to have
a future—

and a past. "I'm lost, I'm like
a stranger to myself."

"I'm an
unstationary pedestal."

"My marbles are slowly rolling away."

She's thrown out family
photos; no longer recalls

her husband, or her
maiden name. Still, she wants him

to lead her back.

"When am I going to see you?
Are we a long distance apart from one another?"

He wants her back.

He wants her back...

If it took only
not looking back

to lead her back, it would be easy
not to look, not to look

back; but if helping her look
back is the one way he knows to

help her back, then he has to help her
look back.

Where else could she look?

"I'll try not to remember
too many things. I'll just remember

what I can..."

Do we (don't we) have more (he wishes he
knew) than what we can look back to?

Times at Bellosguardo

*translated from the Italian
by Jonathan Galassi*

Oh how there in the glittering
stretch that bends toward the hills
the hum of evening lessens
and the trees chat with the hackneyed
murmur of the sand; and how this common life
no more our own than our breath
gets channeled there, crystalline,
into orders of columns
and willows at the edges
and great *ha-ha*s in the gardens
by the overbrimming basins,
and how a sapphire light returns
for the men who live down there:
it is too sad
such peace should enlighten in glimmers
and everything then roll on, with a few flashes
over the steaming riverbends,
with intersecting chimneys
and shouts from the hanging gardens
and consternation and long laughter
over patched roofs, among the arrases
of massed branches and a brilliant tail
that trails across the sky before
desire can find the words!

* * *

Forlorn on the hill
brown-green magnolia
boughs, when the wind
arouses a troubled
agitation of chords

from the frigidaria
of the ground floors
and every leaf that sways
or flares back in the thicket
drinks that greeting in
in every fiber;
and more forlorn, the limbs
of the living that get lost
in the prism of the minute,
fevered limbs devoted
to motion that goes on
and on in its small round:
sweat that throbs, sweat of death,
mirrored acts and minutes
that never change, refracting
echoes of the beating up above
that facets sun and rain,
swift swaying between life
that goes and life that stays,
no escape up here: we die
knowing or else choose
chameleon, heedless life: another death.
And the way descends
among loggias and herms: the chord
stirs the stones that have seen
the great images, honor,
unbending love, the test,
unchanging faithfulness.
And the gesture remains: it measures
the emptiness, sounds its limits:
the unknown motion that describes
itself and nothing else: eternal
passion in a blood and brain
that won't return: and maybe
it enters the close and breaks
the lock with its fine pick.

* * *

The clatter of the roof tiles, shattered by
the storm
in the expanded air that doesn't crack,
the bending of the three-point
Canada poplar that shivers
in the garden at every gust—and the sign:
of a life that accords with the marble
at every step, the way the ivy
shrinks from the solitary thrust
of bridges I can make out from this height;
of an hourglass measuring not sand
but works and human faces, human plants;
of water calm under follies,
no longer raging to explore the pumice
grottoes—is it gone?
A long sound comes from the tiles, the stakes
barely hold up the morning glories' coils,
and the locusts that rained
from the arbors onto the books limp off;
hard labor, heavenly weavers, interrupted
on the loom of men. And tomorrow...

A Christmas Story

All dressed up in the back
of a taxi stopped at a traffic
light on Central Park West

one cocktail hour in December,
I happened to spot a pair
of shoes dangling in the air—

brown, clownish workshoes dancing
like marionettes from the thick
strings of their knotted laces,

which somebody (with a ladder?)
had slung across the highest
bare bough of a tree.

Tongues out, their eyelets popping,
mimes enacting a desperate
hilarity or disaster,

they reeled, each time a gust
of wind knocked their heads together,
at the naked, shivering business

of living however we must:
possessed, or not, of a clue
as to how it was you lost

first this, then the other shoe
of your one and only pair
(a person who mislays

a pair of shoes on the street
is—paradoxically—not
likely to have a spare);

possessed, or not, of a guess
as to where you should start to look,
or whether the clever soul

who hung your shoes like a star
on a Christmas tree, too far
up to be any use,

had wanted to help you out.
Three-faced, the traffic light
turned green and swayed in doubt.

Brief Candle

The funicular, effortless
  as a toy, glides humming to a stop
halfway uphill. Teeming with tourists, the steps
  break halfway again at a terrace
where we pause to catch our breath, and half of Paris—

  though today, in the August haze,
  the view from Montmartre is just the odd
tin rooftop the sun's dropped match sets ablaze,
  the gilded dome of Les Invalides,
the pipe dream of the Pompidou. Should these

  not do, dozens of Eiffel
  Towers are glinting at our feet,
each the capital of a shape that repeats
  on the map of a vendor's Persian carpet.
Balloon-sellers, too, a bongo group, a *triste*

  untalented guitarist—
  we rise above them all to enter
buoyantly the dark of Sacré Coeur.
  Christ is still hugely aflame
behind the altar, his heart of gold

  mosaic flickering
  with feeling, his outstretched arms
in a gesture that serves for love and crucifixion.
  And in unison, a hundred hands
reach for candles and a pocketful of change.

  But now a frenzied mob
  behind them is advancing, afraid
the candelabra, tiered like Christmas trees,
  have no room left for one last prayer.
A boy secures his on top, since to be the star

MARY JO SALTER

to him seems natural,
while a girl illumines hers with a can
of Coke aloft in the other hand. All
for nothing: however had we missed
the man whose job is to snuff our wishes out?

That's how space is found:
the instant people turn around,
he picks their candles up by the blazing wicks,
two-fisted, and with blackened thumbs
chucks them into a pail—then the next soul comes,

paying fifteen francs
for the longest kind, which lasts the same
as for those who paid ten or five, or who never came.
Could it be he enjoys this? Or does
he stand there for a divine indifference

to all our pleas and thanks
and the guttering hope we matter? Though
an arrow points the *Sens de la Visite,*
we decide to make our own sense of it
outdoors, in the all-consuming furnace of summer.

And there, choosing to skip
the train, we run into a gypsy
beggar of five or six, who has set up shop
on a step. His cup is empty,
its earnings slipped beneath his rug, or rag,

but he hasn't hid his booty
of big, dirty biscuits, embossed like coins,
which triple as money, food, and toys at once.
From his hands, themselves as sooty
as the man's upstairs, they rise in fragile towers

he demolishes carefully, and over and over.

Samuel Scott's A Sunset, With a View of Nine Elms

At this distance, from the other shore,
looking across the river north and east,
you just can't tell what kind of trees they are,
feathered in those ideal humid greens
in a sort of flow toward the horizon
and the ocean. In perspective they diminish
to depletion, into the sunset's haw
and haze, as if the water had drained
out of them into water, though closer
to the viewer they tower like a cloud.
This may or may not be Cuckold's Point
and Pier—the painter's put in buildings
and boats for reference and to tie the trees
to work—and the two men in the boat riding
the drift are either fishermen or journeymen,
one of whom is standing looking into
the water, while above his head, where the dream
Thames turns away, is Saint Mary's Battersea.

Happiness

Today you're going to hike to the very end
Of this steep valley, where the path rises
And disappears beyond the waterfall
Marked on the yellow sign you saw last night
Before you went to sleep to dream of today.
Now, as you yawn here on the balcony
Of the chalet, you hear distant cowbells.
Clouds drift off to reveal the mighty glacier
Glittering in the folds of limestone peaks.
The fields around you are already half in sun,
Spangled with cow parsley and blue flowers,
So pinch yourself. This isn't a dream at all.
Go on, take that crooked path by the monastery,
And cross the meadow where the brothers' cows
Browse near the haystacks. Let the morning dew
Brush against your legs, and don't be afraid
Of distracted bees who come to smell your pollen.
Your path winds up among the wild flowers,
Brilliant carpets of purple and yellow stars
Cut by the flash of swiftly running streams.
Don't forget to open and shut each gate,
And greet the cows cropping the high pastures
Below the moraine. You can rest on a boulder
As big as a house, swept down years ago
From waves of ice bright on the ridge above,
But you must keep walking to the valley's end,
Ignoring the signs for trails that lead to summits
Crowded with tourists riding the cable car,
Beer gardens, grottos, or sculptured ice caves.
You're heading for that wall of windswept granite
Already casting a shadow over the fields
Where bony cows graze on the last, thin grass,
And when you arrive, you'll shiver with pleasure,

Delighted by the small, whitewashed chapel,
And the farmhouse close to the famous pass
Where a herder's family eats at a trestle table
Under an apple tree. But you must be careful
As you approach. This is the one moment
When happiness could be blown from your grasp
Like a child's balloon, so you must guard it,
Not release it with a sigh or a groan
By looking up above the waterfall,
And wishing you could cross the dangerous pass.
You have no grappling hooks. It's getting cold.
That's fog blowing in sheets over the ridge,
Thunder booming from the vanished gorge.
Now you must bravely turn your back forever
On the outskirts of what's impossible,
And return without regret to your calm life,
Content to remember your long, perfect day.
For if you start to climb that perilous trail
As I see you doing now, your smile gone,
Your heart pounding as you brace your shoulders,
Determined to find a way up through the mist,
Who will follow you, who will lead you back?

Ben Nevis

*"Read me a lesson, Muse, and speak it loud
Upon the top of Nevis, blind in mist!"*

Did Keats sit here or there
to write his sonnet? The chasm
drops away. Below the air
shimmers with auto exhaust

and hikers strip off shirts,
pinking their backs in the sun.
I've climbed a shadeless trail
sweating and gasping

with hundreds of other people
coming up from the car park,
fathers in bill caps, mothers
tugging children by the hand,

old men, red-faced and wobbly
leaning on ski poles, everyone
sharing inadequate water
surprised by such violent heat

so that some cupped their hands
in falling stream trickles
below sheep folds. I thought
I was climbing out of Hell

until I reached the top.
The hotel had not been built
when Keats slogged up here;
now it's already a ruin,

a pile of tumbled-down rocks
filled with lager cans,
biscuit wrappers, toilet paper—
the world's ugliest summit,

rocks and debris, sewer pipe,
dirty patches of snow,
and, from a pitched orange tent,
amplified drums, screamed lyrics.

August 2, 1818—yearning
for the Beautiful, sad Keats
chafed his cold hands,
blinded by the Scottish mist,

and remembered Burns's cottage:
"O the flummery of a birth place!
Cant! Cant! Cant!"
This is what he'd longed for,

his own peak in Darien,
grandeur and shortness of breath
mixed up until he felt dizzy
like a long night reading Homer.

He stepped nearer the edge
where the cliff disappeared
into a cloud, or was it steam
rising up from a lake in Hell?

Alarmed, Brown called him back
and he turned, shuddering,
not yet daring to hear
an answer from the sullen mist.

So he sat down, his throat sore,
took off his stiff boots,
and dutifully smoothed paper
over his knee. And wrote.

Negative Capability

Soft, dead rain and raw.
Fingers of asparagus halted,
dandelions pinched in a slate
lace of failed snow, air loaded
with undelivered light.
Lovely, a pleasure
to step back on the weak sod

into the last century (old as this one is)
behind the whackily settled house, ell and barn
to the tipsy, heaved outhouse, and through its skinny door.
The bony smell of winter isn't news
in the whitewashed walls, necrosed magazines: *Collier's,*
Saturday Evening Post, National Geographic, and books:
Temples of Convenience, New England Indian Summer,
Twentieth Century Pleasures, Duino Elegies,
racked beneath the lunar roll.

No real relief in going.
Just pleasure, "... the capability of submission."
The last of any congregation
needn't confess, any more than the first,
though this *is* the place for it, the door wide open
despite the bimonthly meter man, illegal clammer
headed for the toxic flats, rare, daytime
lovers on a dead-end road,
who might glance between the scabby, shingled buildings
"timelessly" framed by this doorway:
dumb as Wyeth's cripple
yearning in an August field, his
dories turtled on a gravel beach.
Failures of feeling? Yes, but this is a source
of mild joy, this chilled time of year, infused

with the faintly sweet, sick harbor fog
seeping in with the imperfectly known.

July glares: black-eyed Susan, fuchsia fireweed, lime
grass and chartreuse hay, willow whip and torchy
Indian paintbrush . . . the explosive 4th,
children of guests, sky-blue sedans with lilac gawkers,
red Cherokees, motor homes looking for land
at the old prices, UPS, mail,
the Wolper, like an orange *mantis religioso,*
poised in roadside alder, waiting to grade the road,
diesels inland, Gregorian through their gears, chanting on Rt. 1,
lobster boats on the bay, grumbling, jets like tinsel,
trails evaporating, metaphysical,
the clank of chain and pail in the stone well
while someone new
has an original experience with water.
The dogs snooze in the cool,
packed dirt under the woodshed
away from the panic of blackflies, the antic children,
Labor Day weeks away.
I shut the door.

It's like the atmosphere of Saturn then,
red Stygian hibiscus
blooming behind my beaded lids.
There are three holes in the world.
I've plugged one; the other two
sigh over the leeching pit. It's wonderful,
past dying, buried alive in the landfill
under gravid plastic bags, all-American
suffocation in soured cultural awareness . . .
beneath me, generations of ruptured
horsehair sofas, Colonial aspirations
gone methane. A committee of flies
sucked in as I shut the door,
harmonic particulates of atmosphere
that would have delighted Emily,
who let herself get down to one.

But the melancholic cool of April
doesn't stir my guts.
What I have is enough
cold crap to keep me straighter
than Ecclesiastes, that benign
hypocrite, still giddy on Isaiah's fumes.
I am willing to leave everything to
the future.

Of course I come out of my closet,
into summer, onto the hot, battered path,
blinking and able among you all.
But I remember April,
charnel as its gibbous morning moon,
memento mori, gray as this century,
its fullness over, baring itself
on a nineteenth-century peg.

John Keats in Colorado

for Leslie and Kitty Norris

He has no choice: he must leave England
and travel, not to Rome, a mistake in his case,
but to Colorado where the mountain air
and winter sun will clear his lungs.
He'll pack a twig from the plum tree
and some gravel from the garden walk.
He'll sing to himself the nightingale's song.
A lock of Fanny Brawne's hair and the hope
that she'll follow, he'll carry with him
across the ocean, across the continent.
He'll bring some of his leatherbound books.
In the afternoon, where the sun streams
through the window, he'll sit and read.
He won't think he's home—
home is Hampstead and the stucco house
with its tall windows where he stood
looking out at the rain falling in the garden,
himself falling in love with Fanny
and hearing the rasp of his breath,
seeing the brightness of his blood.
High in the Colorado mountains,
he'll long for home but out of the difference
he'll heal and live for years writing
about the hunting songs of coyotes
and the revelations of the frontier.
Fanny will travel by stage to Denver
and together they'll ride down the valley
between mountain ranges to a new home.
She'll bake his grandmother's plum cake
for Twelfth Night festivities and the house

will be redolent of nutmeg and rum.
Falling asleep under Colorado skies,
he'll hear in dreams the songs
of the coyote and the nightingale,
how they haunt mountainside and heath.

Lawrence

On two occasions in the past twelve months
I have failed, when someone at a party
spoke of him with a dismissive scorn,
to stand up for D. H. Lawrence,

a man who burned like an acetylene torch
from one end to the other of his life.
These individuals, whose relationship to literature
is approximately that of a tree shredder

to stands of old-growth forest,
these people leaned back in their chairs,
bellies full of dry white wine and the ovum of some foreign fish,
and casually dropped his name

the way pygmies with their little poison spears
strut around the carcass of a fallen elephant.
"O Elephant," they say,
"you are not so big and brave today!"

It's a bad day when people speak of their superiors
with a contempt they haven't earned,
and it's a sorry thing when certain other people

don't defend the great dead ones
who have opened up the world before them.
And though, in the catalogue of my betrayals,
this is a fairly minor entry,

I resolve, if the occasion should recur,
to uncheck my tongue and say, "I love the spectacle
of maggots condescending to a corpse,"
or, "You should be so lucky in your brainy, bloodless life

as to deserve to lift
just one of D. H. Lawrence's urine samples
to your arid psychobiographic
theory-tainted lips."

Or maybe I'll just take the shortcut
between the spirit and the flesh,
and punch someone in the face,
because human beings haven't come that far

in their effort to subdue the body,
and we still walk around like zombies
in our dying, burning world,
able to do little more

than fight, and fuck, and crow,
something Lawrence wrote about
in such a manner
as to make us seem magnificent.

Cavalcanti's Dream: World's End

I walked the curving, mercury stairway
    Spiraling far beyond the moon
        In its languid way never meant

For men. There I saw how we'd be left
    Only Mary's stained & ancient veils, unfolding
        Before us as slowly as sails

On our way to the rendezvous beneath the tower
    Where black clouds rippled closely
        As the hour. Those soft, wooden slats

Of the drawbridge rails... still torn
    Delicately as flesh by random nails; the sky
        Itself printed with God's seal, that

Festering white eye, mute zero ablaze with fire,
    Wheeling out the fate of the faithful as they kneel...
        A world lost until some final future

Sin, when the heart stands able to begin again.

Laura Providencia in the New World

High up, in the towers of the public housing project, Laura Providencia and her mother, her brother, Angel, and her little sister, Rosita, lived under siege. In the elevator that smelled like a urinal, the junkies bobbed devotionally. The walls of the long hallways teemed with the exploding alphabet, the declamations, white, screaming, "Paco of St. Ann's Ave," "Hector El Corazón," "The Bishops," the worm-like letters spawning words, the words clamoring over one another, keeping pace with Laura Providencia as she walked down the long hallway toward the vestibule where the mailboxes were plundered.

During the first months in the new country, she had longed for letters from her cousins on the island to corroborate what she thought she remembered. She learned the new language quickly and felt all at once like a guest in her own life. Laura's mother, Señora Milagros, was astonished, and suspected that the rapidity with which her daughter learned the new language was symptomatic of some unnameable contagion of the barbarous new world. Although, in the new world, shoes were plentiful. Stunned, Señora Milagros looked at the dark girl budding into a woman, the pretty girl mouthing with such facility the noise of the new incomprehensible words, and she forgot the occasion of Laura Providencia's fourteenth birthday. But Angel, who was one year older than his sister, celebrated his birthday on the same day, and as Señora Milagros remembered her son's birthday, it seemed to her that Laura had loitered in her womb as a reproach for the passion that had made her.

Señora Milagros regaled her neighbor, Señora Ramirez, with the story: she told it tenderly, and Laura knew she was meant to overhear, as God was meant to overhear. "*Dios mío*, a day and a night in labor, the pain like knives, she came out of my body, tore me to pieces. I was nursing her brother, and she was not supposed to happen; but she was in me, growing, and dried up the milk in my breasts. I had to hire my cousin Teresa to nurse Angel. I paid

Teresa with my shoes. After a year to the day her brother was born, she came. And then this one," Señora Milagros said, caught her breath, and braced her back against the couch pillow. She spread the fingers of her large right hand, held and encompassed the top of Rosita's velvety head. Señora Ramirez said, "*Pero, pero,*" her hands twitched in her lap, her face disfigured with a disappointment as profound as a child's; she struggled against the desire to weep, shocked by the audacity that had compelled her to interrupt Señora Milagros.

Laura Providencia noticed that the women's gestures mirrored one another: they sighed in harmony, and breathed in unison, the black-sheathed, swelling cushions of their breasts a rising tide of dark moons obscuring their chins. But they weren't identical, though Laura had seen them that way; except now, the crack, the sudden momentary fissure in Laura Providencia's vision precipitated by Señora Ramirez's interrupting "But, but," allowed Laura to see again that her mother's face was round and brown and Señora Ramirez's was teak-colored and narrow, but these distinctions did not alter what the two women found in the greater affinity, their one fate. But it was up to Señora Milagros to tell it; this, Señora Ramirez could not do, she was not the talker, it was up to Lucia Milagros to tell the truth of her heart which was their one life, uniting them deeper than blood. Lucia Milagros telling it, and Dolores Ramirez nervously attentive, until finally she was still, and only listening, and at home in her silence. And now in telling it, Señora Milagros had elected to leave out a part, didn't say it—without explanation, discarding perhaps, foreshortening maybe. Was this all that was left out of the recitation to be tacitly understood, could such a telling be trusted? Out of the wreckage of Señora Ramirez's trance fell language that was all distress, even as her body paid homage, duplicating every movement and gesture of Señora Milagros's.

Señora Ramirez's mouth labored, her tongue slowly hefting one word at a time, attempting to place each word in a coherent order, and, failing, she held up two fingers. Señora Ramirez nodded. Señora Milagros sighed and nodded and told once more of the two children who had died: one in the womb, that she had known was a boy because her belly had come to a point, and she, who had been pretty, became ugly within a month, which was as long as that son had survived within her; and Luz Divina, the infant girl deserted by life after only a week on the earth, taken while napping in her little hammock, without cause or reason that God would reveal to the midwife or priest, all fathered by Noel, who appeared almost as regularly as Christmas. Señora Milagros shrugged and was silent. Señora Ramirez searched Señora Milagros's face for the cause of the altered narrative. Had her friend discovered that she needed to keep some part of the story for herself? Señora Ramirez, who would never presume to tell it, offered the names of her living children, Dolores, Rafael, and Venus (named for the popular song, long before anyone knew that the girl would have the face of a Pekingese dog). Señora Ramirez's face closed as though she were submerging her head beneath water, and for a perfect minute her face became the mask of an enduring Pietà; saying more would achieve nothing, and her friend, her sister in misfortune, knew and didn't need to be told again. Venus, the adolescent girl with the dog's face, hated her mother, and she hated her name: the name that clung to her long after the song ceased to be heard from the windows of the housing project, and there was no point in telling Venus that her mother hadn't intended the irony that adhered to her name like a chronic illness. Venus looked at her mother and couldn't imagine anyone's innocence.

Señora Ramirez's silence puffed out her lips and turned the lobes of her ears red; the silence she kept as long as she could hold her breath wheezed. She gulped air and didn't name the two children she had lost, but genuflected once for each, let out a howl that burst open her mouth, and called "Julio, Julio," not because she expected the man who had fathered her children to ever appear again, but calling out the provisional name she had given to her loss might prime the recitation Señora Milagros had stunted. "Julio, Julio, *mi vida,*" she called.

Señora Milagros said, "*Entonces,* well, Noel was merely useless as other men, he could never understand why any more should be required of him except to be handsome and in love, although he aspired to be dangerous, but was only brutal in manly commonplace ways. Luz Divina who lived only a week was the most beautiful of my children, her face a sublime version of her father's. I mourned for that child six years. During the six years of mourning, Noel's long absences and brief visitations began: during the rare visitations he claimed his husbandly rights. More memorable than Noel's appearances were the soups that my sister Titi prepared and fed me, deepening my sleep. One scalding afternoon, after the hot bath my sister prescribed, and a bowl of her steaming soup, which had the head of a whiskered fish in it, but smelled of jasmine, and had the taste of the best Spanish brandy, my sister Titi helped me into the hammock, strung up in the cement whitewashed bedroom, between two open windows, where one could watch the blue air boil. I breathed out the fumes of the soup, which tickled my temples, swung in the hammock in pursuit of a breeze, slipped out of my sweat-soaked body, and sunk into the most refreshing siesta of my life. At first I didn't recognize the voice as my mother's, it was the voice of a young woman, for whom death did not yet exist. The voice brought with it, from beyond the grave, a cooling breeze, and when she said, 'Pay attention,' I knew it was Mother, the easy and confident way she took authority was unmistakably Mama. The cooling breeze from somewhere else bathed me, and I was aware of never before having been so effortlessly attentive, and then Luz Divina said to me, in the calmest and sweetest voice, 'Mami, don't mourn anymore, six years is sufficient; if I had lived longer, your suffering would have been inconsolable, because at the age of six, in New York of America, I would have been struck by an automobile and killed, and then your pain would have been unsupportable. Mami, do not mourn for me any longer.' And at that time, I'd never had any idea of coming to the United States."

Laura Providencia watched the last tremors ripple at the top of Señora Ramirez's bosom. Her hands opened in her lap, and her face resolved itself into an inconsolable autumnal softness. Laura noted that her mother hadn't significantly altered the catechism of narrative, she had only paused and reordered the sequence in which she spoke of her children. She concluded as always—patted Rosita's head, and said, "And then this one, who now has," and she raised both hands, raising five fingers of her right hand, one finger of her left, one digit at a time, took a breath, and said, "six years." Rosita fidgeted, waiting. Laura stroked her little sister's thin arm, kissed her cheek, and whispered, "Don't worry." Laura thought of how it was easiest for her mother to express affection for Luz Divina. Laura recalled a past when she had envied this sister she had never seen, but now she merely thought of Luz Divina as one of the family; and Rosita's unhappiness had grown more insistent. Laura Providenicia's caresses and explanations calmed the child for briefer intervals. Laura could see Rosita's face working, consuming the poor fictions and caresses she had reached for, and would reach for again, before feeding these comforts to her agitation. Laura knew what Rosita was waiting for, and she knew it wasn't going to happen.

Rosita, thin and brown as a fistful of twigs, at the center of the trembling pink ball of the dress, pushed, and Señora Milagros's hand flew from the top of Rosita's head to her own mouth, to catch and cup the small frightened laugh. The stem of Rosita's neck and her scrawny shoulders shuddered; she pushed her head between her mother's huge knees, which looked to Laura like shrouded boulders about to part, as if Rosita were trying to return to the place of her making; but Laura knew that wasn't it, it was only the long waiting, the endless waiting that had commenced on the day they had left the island, after her mother had told Rosita they were going to visit somebody special. Rosita thought they might be going to visit her grandmother; it was, she knew, a long walk and a car ride to Abuela's house. A car would have to be hired—usually this happened after the long walk to Uncle Nestor's village. Laura wondered why her mother never told the children their destination when they went on trips. Always Señora Milagros just took the children out, and they walked and walked and arrived eventually, someplace. Laura had once thought that her mother might have believed that walking about without knowing the destination would give them the feeling of freedom; or on that day when they left the island, not telling where they were going would obscure the pain of leaving; or maybe her mother thought the children really didn't have to know. Although Laura knew, after a while she figured it out, and Angel knew, too; but Rosita was so little, she became tired of walking and began to cry.

It was a hot, brilliant day. The dust looked like sparks in the sheen of blue air, the ocean beyond the road boomed and gurgled enormously, Rosita's weeping was as distinct and sinuous as the drone of insects hovering about their heads. Señora Milagros stopped in the road, put down and laid open the suitcase at her feet. Rosita plodded to the right of her mother's hip, veered off the road, and stood there, kneading the hem of her dress. Laura Providencia, Angel, and Aunt Titi were strung out in the road not far behind, each weighted with a portion of boxes, bundles, and shopping bags. Aunt Titi bobbed along the road, pressed and scoured into her sacramental essence, a little taller than a dwarf. The huge crucifix swinging from her neck, driving her forward, she halted, and her smiling face, which might have been carved out of a plum pit, peeked out from the pyramid of bundles she carried unerringly. Señora Milagros bent over, her eyes on the extravagant horizon of the sea as her hand probed in the suitcase, under the folded bedsheet, felt the smooth warm glass of the sealed jar of holy water, and grasped and brandished a hand mirror in the air, as a magician might pluck a dove from a bystander's dumb ear. She thrust the mirror in front of Rosita's face. "Look child! *Fea!* See how ugly you are when you cry."

The face Rosita saw flashing in the mirror was the gaping face of a fish, just before the sun burst an explosion of silver light from the mirror, and then Rosita could see nothing, and she wanted to scream, I'm blind, but the scream cracked in her throat, and even after Angel had swept her up, and the world came back into her eyes after the successive blinding blows of silver, and blackness, she knew it all could be taken away, immediately, anytime; and many years later as a middle-aged woman, as she told it all to Laura Providencia, Laura still providing the words, so that she could tell it, Rosita remembered living in an infinite and inexhaustible longing, this recollected as the centuries of someone's childhood she had been told about. But anyway, it was true, she said, that despite the wanted and unwanted attention of men throughout her life, and much testimony to the contrary, she knew herself to be ugly. Although Laura Providencia had helped her to say it, she shook her head, no, no; Rosita shrugged and smiled.

They paused in the road parallel to the sea. The surf boomed and hissed. Skittering blotches of green neon—spit out from the sea—moved on the white sand toward the road and defined themselves as crabs as they crawled out of the glaring light. Aunt Titi gestured for Angel to load his bundles into her arms. Angel obeyed, and divided his bundles and boxes between Aunt Titi and

Laura. He could not deny Aunt Titi what she asked for, any more than he doubted her capacity to carry the load. She had planted this belief in him, and in Laura, long before the children could resist belief, long before belief required effort. She, Aunt Titi, Titi diminutive for Tía, Tía Titi, which became Aunt Titi in the United States, but always she had been known as Auntie, even in some past when she must have been a child, although neither Laura nor Angel could imagine that; but Aunt Titi in the long ago had not so much told them as allowed Laura and Angel to be in the presence of her soliloquies, which said nuns were married to God, and she, Titi, was betrothed to God, forever. Giddy as a Pentecostal with the thought of the end of the world, she'd mentioned the care of this niece, that nephew, her younger sister, Lucia Milagros, so-and-so who's dying, and the still nameless she assisted in being born, all of this merely an aspect of her devotion; and Angel and Laura marveled at her abiding contentment.

Angel hung a shopping bag from the crook of Aunt Titi's elbow and stacked parcels in her arms up to her eyes. Aunt Titi, in her devotions, and under the weight of her burdens, grew smaller and smaller, happy finally to disappear altogether in the service of God.

They continued. Angel carried Rosita. Rosita's skinny legs swung, her sandaled feet bouncing off Angel's thighs. Laura Providencia walked alongside, carrying her pile of boxes and purring at Rosita's ear. Rosita, in Angel's arms, her head on his shoulder, kept her eyes opened and whined. Up ahead, Señora Milagros marched under her load of belongings, and in the rear, a motley of parcels jiggled and moved inexorably down the road, behind and under which, Angel and Laura knew, was Aunt Titi.

They arrived in Uncle Nestor's village. Uncle Nestor, the youngest and most obliging of Aunt Titi and Señora Milagros's brothers, made the arrangements for the hired car and drove them to the airport.

Handsome Uncle Nestor examined his mustache in the rearview mirror, stroking with his forefinger the black lushness of hair on his lip, and navigated the automobile with the barest touch of the steering wheel with his left hand. The car careened and screeched down the mountain road. Inside, amid their tumbling belongings, Uncle Nestor's dog, El Capitán, who traveled everywhere with Nestor, howled. Aunt Titi, Señora Milagros, Angel, Rosita, and Laura Providencia collided, bounced, and bobbled. Rosita screamed. Angel was fascinated by El Capitán. The animal appeared to have been bred from a Russian wolfhound and a goat. Angel, swaying and bouncing, applauded the acrobatic dexterity of El Capitán. The dog managed to remain upright on the floor of the car, his four shivering legs scrabbling in perpetual motion, seemingly sustained by the legato of his wolf howl. The rainbow-hued mountains and God's gaudy sky fell with them in the side windows of the car hurtling toward cataclysm. Angel looked out of the window at the flamboyant mountains in the distance, heard the screeching tires at the edge of nowhere; the sun's light gleamed in the windows, and Angel imagined the long fall, deep enough to confound all physics, far enough to have one's life pass before one's eyes, suffer remorse for the life lived, and enjoy the disorientation of one's first evening in eternity, before ever hitting bottom. The car spiraled down and down. Uncle Nestor, happy and calm, almost succeeded in taking his attention away from the vision of his face in the mirror.

When the car had come down from the mountain and they were hurtling along the long flat road, El Capitán stopped howling. Rosita was still screaming. Señora Milagros turned in the front seat and made a motion with her hands, as if she were going to take the mirror from the suitcase and thrust it in front of Rosita's face again. Rosita stuck her fingers in her mouth, stifled the scream, and gagged. Aunt Titi fished in the shopping bag between her legs, pulled out a melon, an orange, a pink bow of shiny fabric, and a hairbrush. Aunt Titi gave Angel the melon, Laura the orange, and put the glistening pink bow in Rosita's lap. Titi began to brush Rosita's black hair, the slow powerful strokes yanking Rosita's head back. Rosita cried. Titi fixed the pink bow in Rosita's hair and said, "One must suffer to be beautiful." Laura Providencia knew that the point was not beauty, but the virtue in pain. Rosita threw up.

They stopped the car, fetched buckets of seawater, and cleaned up the mess. They stripped Rosita, standing in the road, Aunt Titi, Señora Milagros, and Laura Providencia shielding the near-naked child from the sight of Angel and Uncle Nestor. El Capitán ran in circles and barked. Uncle Nestor held his nose and strolled beyond the range of the bad smell. El Capitán ran after him. Aunt Titi opened one parcel, removed various herbs and ingredients she had named but whose names she would not share, and brewed the special tea for Rosita. The heat of the day was such that Titi did not need a fire to cook the ingredients; she poured the tea from a jar into a baby bottle, snapped on the rubber nipple, and vigorously shook the contents.

Rosita stood, washed and in a clean frock, near a palm tree, whose shade was obliterated by the noon-day heat, and sucked the bottle dry.

Back in the car Angel cradled her. When they reached the airport, Rosita was still sleeping. Laura Providencia said, "Look, Rosita, an airplane! We are going to fly." Rosita snored. Angel carried Rosita on the plane. Once during the flight, Rosita's eyes flickered. Rosita awoke in Nueva York, America.

"I want to go home." Rosita was waiting, still waiting. Señora Ramirez reached over and stroked Rosita's head. It seemed to Rosita that her mother, through her meanderings, had misplaced home, as she must have misplaced the man who was her father.

This, at least, was what Laura thought Rosita was trying to say, as Laura retrieved her little sister's words, one at a time, from the wet, hiccuping sobs. "And this one," Señora Milagros said, tugging down the heavy folds of her dress and lifting Rosita's chin from her lap, "this one is never still."

Later, in the sketch Laura would make of Señora Ramirez and her mother, and hide in her closet, Laura depicted the two women as nearly identical, the women's ballooned and shapeless childbearing bodies shrouded in the black, sack-like dresses. Laura's mother wore the heavy woolen dress with the thick, abrasive rope around where her waist used to be. From the rope's two ends hung two large weighted knots, each shaped like the clapper in a church bell.

After the third month in the United States, Laura's mother had asked Laura if she would wear the heavy black dress, and the rope, for a while. Señora Milagros explained that now that Laura was a señorita, having menstruated, she could help pay some of the debt that her mother owed to Our Lady of Perpetual Succor. Many years ago, said Señora Milagros, she had promised the saint that if she granted her cousin Teresa, who had once nursed Angel but had, several years later, contracted tuberculosis—if the saint granted Cousin Teresa one more good long year to live, she, Lucia Milagros, would wear the heavy penitential dress for two years in return for the one year granted Cousin Teresa. But, said Señora Milagros, she was still a young person when she made the vow, and not capable of the necessary seriousness; she had only worn the dress five months. She was not sure that the misfortune in her life was due to the unpaid debt to Our Lady of Perpetual Succor, but she felt that the debt had undoubtedly made her susceptible to envious people, and the evil eye. Now she had been wearing the dress for almost a year, and the ponderous rope pulled at her back as she sat at the sewing machine in the factory. The pain in her lower back slowed her hands, and she was being paid, she reminded Laura, on the basis of piecework. So, she said, if Laura who was now a señorita took on a small portion of her debt, for only a couple of months, there would be the relief to Mother's back, and she would bring more money into the house.

Laura knew that when her mother referred to herself in the third person, and invoked the title "Mother," her mother had marshaled the moral force of all creation; and as Laura steeled herself to say no, she felt herself complicit in her mother's martyrdom. Laura's voice shook. She explained again that she couldn't wear the dress to school. Señora Milagros frowned. Laura said that although such a costume was not expressly forbidden, it was inappropriate. Laura offered to wear the penitential dress during the summer, when she was not attending school. Her mother said, "In the summer I will not need you, by then my debt will have been paid."

Rosita fidgeted in Laura's arms. Laura pressed her cheek to Rosita's temple and tightened her embrace. Looking out from the periphery of Rosita's hot brow, Laura's vision lingered for an instant on the smear of pink icing on her mother's mouth. Señora Milagros looked into Laura's face, and saw what Laura was seeing; Señora Milagros's eyes went black and accusatory, as if Laura's seeing was itself a mockery. Laura felt suddenly like a child caught in a shameful act; she managed not to blurt out that it was Angel's fault. He had handed the plates of birthday cake to his mother and Señora Ramirez and run off. It was, after all, his birthday cake, and of course he was gone, out in the street. Laura felt again the presence of his absence, the weight of it in her chest, and then she wanted to apologize to him, too, for the readiness of her heart to heap blame on him. What did it matter that it was the icing on his cake that had smeared Mama's mouth with the gaudiness? Laura spoke. "But Mama," she said, "but," and was startled by the sound of her own voice, which she recognized as her own, although it sounded false to her. She reminded herself that she had not denounced her brother, and she made cooing noises in Rosita's ear.

Señora Milagros, with her thumb and pinkie, deftly pinched the corners of her mouth, and the blotches of pink icing disappeared. She looked down at her well-shod feet, and when Señora Milagros looked up again, Laura saw on her mother's face something like confirmation, a look benign and tantamount to forgiveness; she had almost smiled.

In that first year, Rosita had begun the first grade, and the black girls beat her up. Laura talked to her mother about the hazards of the public school. Children not much older than Rosita were seen making deliveries of drugs in the schoolyard. Señora Milagros had heard of the thirteen-year-old expectant mothers who would not complete the seventh grade. Señora Milagros and Aunt Titi decided on St. Ann's School for Rosita.

Laura delivered Rosita into the custody of the nuns. Nothing in the street frightened Rosita as much as the sisters at St. Ann's School. Laura had turned away from the sight of the nun in the arched doorway, and all she could remember of the nun's face was that it was an inspiration to abstinence and chastity of every kind, and Laura did not wish to see the face again. The school and the church attached to it were the only buildings left standing on the street. Beyond the church and the gray mortuary stone of the school and its fenced-in box of graveled yard was rubble and the smoke-blackened walls of burnt-out buildings.

Rosita hung on to the wrought-iron fence in front of the school. She sat down, bunched, and anchored herself on the sidewalk; her small fists clutched around the iron bars were difficult to get at through the barrier she had made of her hunched upper body. Laura struggled. She reached in through the crevice between Rosita's upper arm and forearm, and tried to work Rosita's fingers loose. Laura pleaded. Rosita whimpered. Other children, parents, filed past them and said nothing. Laura begged; she pulled at Rosita's shoulder, wedging Rosita a little way from the fence. Rosita clung, her fists knotted around the iron bars. Laura heard herself wail, and she ran from the sight of Rosita clutching the fence, from the nun whose face neither she nor Rosita wanted to see moving out from under the arched doorway.

Laura ran, and remembered Rosita rising obediently from the sidewalk and following the nun into the school, although Laura could not have seen this, running as she was, not wanting to see. But when she remembered it, she remembered always Rosita letting go, rising with a look of sudden forbearance on her face, and following the nun into the school. Laura Providencia described it this way in memory, as over the years Rosita forgave her sister again and again.

The white lady with blue hair had come to their house. She was a very tall, thin old lady with a dignified and kindly face. Laura answered the door. She thought that Miss Hamilton resembled a great white bird, a bird bringing her the fulfillment of her dearest wish; she would attend a school where she would be required to do what made her happiest, draw pictures for hours on end. Señora Milagros and Aunt Titi thought of Laura's drawing as an aspect of her tendency for inattentiveness, an eccentricity that could become a vice, if left unattended, but here was this woman of great dignity who had come to their home, the white woman with blue hair, whose tremulous and patrician voice was itself blue. Aunt Titi did not understand a word the blue-haired, blue-voiced old white woman said, but felt and knew an immediate and deep affinity for the magisterial, chaste presence who had honored them by coming to their door. Before Laura was allowed to translate for Miss Hamilton, the dean of student affairs at the High School of Music and Art, Laura's mother and aunt sent Laura hurrying off with a glance at Laura's bare feet.

In the dark closet, Laura studied the long seam of light in the crack of the slightly opened door, waiting and knowing that the light would tell her nothing beyond the possibilities of its design and radiance. She stood in the dark and fondled the everyday shoes cradled in her arms; she had put her special Sunday patent leather shoes on her feet. She knew she had injured her mother and Aunt Titi by answering the door and admitting Miss Hamilton into the house while she was still barefoot. A letter had come from the school announcing the time and date of Miss Hamilton's visit and asking if the designated time for the visit was convenient. But Laura Providencia and her mother and aunt had trouble in believing in what the letter said, believing that it could happen, and so they forgot about it; or, on Laura's part, not so much forgetting the portentous visit as placing the time of the visit in some messianic future that could never be imminent.

Through the crack in the slightly opened closet door and its seam of light, Laura breathed in the powerful hospital smell of the disinfectant her mother had insisted Laura use when she washed the floors. Suddenly Laura was certain that Miss Hamilton had seen the drawing she had made of the immaculate grotto that was her home. The drawing was one of the twelve Laura had submitted in a portfolio to the entrance committee. In the drawing, Laura had rendered with colored inks the living room and the peach-colored wall where the flock of pink tin cherubim ascended toward the thorn-crowned bleeding Jesus pointing to his heart in flame. Down, diagonally from the cherubim, on a transparent plastic console, in which a three-dimensional waterfall cascaded beneath a flickering rainbow, a flock of doves, whose wings beat to the mysterious tides of light in the transparent console, supported a large tank of tropical fish. The gloriously colored bits of living flesh darted about in the water, a miniature glass castle, wrecked schooner, and a thumb-sized mermaid with silver breasts imbedded in an ocean floor of candy-colored marbles. Adjacent to the underwater life which was stacked above the waterfall, and past the television set and the clock on the wall—a smiling sun with golden spokes supporting neon stars—was the altar loaded with votive candles, the profusion of small erect flames spuming thin scrolls of smoke, surrounding a foot-high statue of the Virgin Mary.

The composition of the drawing suggested an inventory of the too-fecund miracle of creation, threatening to overwhelm the hallowed space where one might pray. It was funny. Laura had not known the drawing would be funny when she began sketching the sun clock with the radiating spokes and stars her mother had purchased at the five-and-ten, but when she completed the drawing, she had smiled. She was, after she thought about it, tempted to destroy the drawing, but she could not. She included it in her entrance portfolio. Now in the dark closet she heard her mother and her aunt offering Miss Hamilton coffee, and Miss Hamilton, not understanding a word, making flattering statements about their home, which neither her mother nor her aunt understood; and her mother and aunt were calling "Laura, Laura Providencia, *por favor.*" Laura decided not to bring her everyday shoes into the living room to display what her aunt and mother provided; the patent leather shoes on her feet were sufficient. But she came out of the closet knowing she had exposed a nakedness, revealed something of the inner life of her family in a way that the living room itself, and her mother and aunt, standing there, could not. In the walk from the bedroom to the living room, Laura had time to change her mind several times. First she concluded that she was not really guilty of betraying her family. What her drawing revealed was something she had not known or intended, and she was, she told herself, as surprised as any stranger to discover what the completed drawing revealed; but there was something else she could not exonerate herself from, and it festered and thrilled her. The blue-haired white lady carried some idea of who Laura Providencia might be; Laura didn't know exactly what the idea was, but she suspected that it must be something grand and fine, and Laura knew she had given the picture she had made, the blatantly funny picture of where her family lived, in partial payment for the wonderful idea the white lady with blue hair had of her, and she had answered the door barefoot.

Señora Milagros, and Titi, Laura Providencia, and Miss Hamilton sat down to coffee. Rosita was napping in her bedroom. Angel was somewhere in the street. Miss Hamilton sipped the inky coffee, and her transparent eyes became avid, while her kindly and dignified smile remained fixed. She said that Laura Providencia was one of three Puerto Rican students accepted at the school. She said that that very day she was going to visit the other two new students, and welcome them to the school; would it be possible, Miss Hamilton wanted to know, for Laura to accompany her to welcome the new students to the school? Laura translated the request. Señora Milagros hesitated. She looked at her sister. Aunt Titi nodded yes. Señora Milagros said, *"Sí."*

Down in the street, the white lady with blue hair moved through the neighborhood like an apparition. Laura felt it was her presence that lent Miss Hamilton visibility.

Laura was surprised by what her innocent and purposeful hand continued to render. She stacked her drawings on the shelf of the closet, under the shoe boxes and above the rail where her Communion dress hung. She knew herself to be alternately innocent and guilty, but mostly innocent, except for the irreducible something in her that saw, and all that her hand made visible, without a trace of charity for the world it made manifest, or the maker, ostensibly herself. Aunt Titi was certain that the old white-white woman's visit was a sign, evidence, and vindication for the journey to the United States. Señora Milagros and Aunt Titi did not say so, would not utter it, who knows what malevolent spirit might be present to overhear, but they nodded furtively in affirmation, and insisted on the present of the new special outfit Laura Providencia would wear to her first day of school.

Angel and Rosita slept. Señora Milagros, Aunt Titi, and Laura Providencia were up most of the night. Laura stood, in her slip, on a kitchen chair. She dressed and undressed many times. Aunt Titi and her mother sewed and altered the various parts of the garment she would wear. Laura Providencia endured their gift. Wearing it, she would be wearing what her eyes saw, what her hand would render, so that if her hand mocked anything, it mocked her also; willing, compliant, accepting the gift, she was not completely apart from what she saw and rendered, and there was, Laura Providencia hoped, some form of dispensation in this. She owed it, as her mother owed time in her penitential dress.

Aunt Titi had traveled downtown to Orchard Street to purchase from two pushcart vendors and Molly's Millinery a pink pillbox hat with a white netted veil, the white elbow-length gloves, and a salmon-colored, cake-shaped purse with shoulder straps, large enough to carry lunch, books, pencils, and a handkerchief. Señora Milagros worked very hard to get the bodice of the dress to fit Laura properly; it was shaped and layered like an artichoke, vibrant green, and would have obscured Laura's waist if not for the tufted, creamy-white sash culminating in a large bow on Laura's thin hip. Aunt Titi stitched on the bow. The skirt flowed down in night-blue velvet pleats, pocked with silver stars; the lace hem of the skirt was circled by a flock of doves, chasing each other around, just above Laura Providencia's feet, which were sheathed in white socks and the Sunday black patent leather shoes.

That morning Señora Milagros and Aunt Titi dressed Laura with great care. Laura stood on the kitchen chair, one white socked foot gracefully extended. Her mother bent beneath her and slipped the gleaming black shoe on Laura's foot. Aunt Titi, just a little taller than the chair Laura stood on, and in a posture that looked like a frozen curtsey, reached up to hold Laura's hand and steady her balance. The early morning light washed over the dark of the kitchen window and turned one shimmering pane into a mirror. Laura perched on the chair, her mother tenderly held one foot, Aunt Titi held her hand. Laura Providencia saw herself mirrored in the kitchen window, gowned as some regal tropical plant, floating above the clotheslines and rooftops she could see through the window. Laura recollected having dozed off and waking surprised many times through the long night. She opened her eyes, and her mother asked her to get undressed, to raise her arms, to turn around, to step down from the chair. Laura stepped down from the chair, her elegant descent mimicking a choreography she could vaguely remember having seen somewhere, perhaps in a movie, or maybe she had read it; and it occurred to her then that she might only be momentarily trapped in her mother's story; but the dress was so heavy.

Señora Milagros slipped the white elbow-length gloves on Laura's outstretched arms. Aunt Titi stood on her tiptoes, holding the pink pillbox-shaped hat with the white netted veil just above Laura Providencia's head. Señora Milagros whispered, *"Esperate."* Laura closed her eyes. Her mother's hands touched her face softly, rubbed her cheeks, caressed her temples and neck. Laura felt the coolness of the cosmetic smeared with the most meticulous care over every inch of her face and neck. She felt her mother's calm breath on her closed eyelids, and knew her mother's belief in this concluding act to be the most she could bestow.

Laura Providencia opened her eyes. Her mother stood an arm's length in front of her, aiming the large hand mirror in which Rosita had seen her face as that of a gaping fish. Laura saw in the mirror that she was white, her caramel-brown face had been turned into a mask of ghostly white. The pink pillbox hat with the white netted veil came down in Titi's hands, crowning her head. Señora Milagros and Aunt Titi applauded softly, and went to awaken Rosita.

Laura Providencia moved down the street under the weight of the garment; in her white gloved hand she clasped Rosita's small hand and tugged her along the sidewalk. She kept up a steady patter of talk, as her little sister seemed to recognize her voice, even as Rosita looked at the strange person with the ghostly white face with suspicion. Laura saw the street—people hurrying towards the subway station—and Rosita through the gauzy film of the netted veil. The whitish haze softened everything she saw, as if the whiteness of her skin were giving off the largesse and privilege of its color, everything seen at a remove and modulated by a mist as subtle as dust.

People rushed by them hurrying to the subway entrance. Laura kept on talking to Rosita, trying to reassure her that she was herself. Rosita glanced at the person holding her hand, tugging her along the sidewalk. Laura could not lift the veil. It hadn't been necessary for her to put words to her tacit understanding; she was under the obligation of a covenant; she would not lift up the veil. When they reached the street of St. Ann's School, Laura was dragging Rosita. Rosita howled. Laura realized that she had lost or left behind the large cake-shaped purse containing her books, pencils, lunch, and handkerchief. She could still feel the phantom weight of the heavy purse's shoulder strap. Rosita was hunkered down, clinging to the wrought-iron fence. Rosita peeked at the ghost face that claimed to be her sister, and at the nun in her black habit with the most forbidding face in the world moving out toward her from under the arched doorway. Laura's scream billowed out the veil curtaining her mouth as she swung; she glimpsed the blood gush from Rosita's nose, and several streets later she saw the blood on her white gloves.

Laura Providencia walked slowly down the long hallway. On either side of her, venerable oaken doors emitted a silence she willed herself to inhabit. The crowd following her was noisy and laughing. A series of bells went off louder than a junkyard of alarm clocks, shrill and persistent in the space of half a minute. Many of the students who had been following her ran off, but many stayed, surrounding her, blocking her path so that Laura couldn't go forward, although she had no clear idea of where she was going. Many of the students were shouting questions at her, some seemed concerned, some were laughing. The old white lady with the blue hair and blue voice broke through the crowd. Her face asked a question. Laura Providencia thought she had said, "Yes, miss," or "Yes, missis, may I help you?" but she wasn't sure. Somehow, through the long walk down the interminable hallways of the school, Laura Providencia had lost her English. The old white lady with the blue hair didn't recognize her. She looked about the crowd to locate the student who might identify this apparently lost elfin parent. Laura clenched the silence in her throat. Miss Hamilton lifted, from the flat terrain of the breast pocket of her tweed gray tunic, a lorgnette, pinned and hanging from a ribbon. She squinted through the lorgnette she held between thumb and forefinger. Bending down, and peering into the face behind the gauzy veil, she exclaimed, "Oh my, my." The white face behind the veil was weeping brown streaks into its whiteness. Laura Providencia threw her white-gloved hands up in front of her face. Miss Hamilton saw the blood-stained palms. She touched Laura's arms, looking for injury. She fluttered her hands and spoke kindly and authoritatively in her blue voice, and the students dispersed.

Miss Hamilton led Laura by the hand through one of the oaken doors with a pebbled opaque window. In the women's faculty bathroom, Miss Hamilton removed the pink veiled hat from Laura's head and put it on a stool. She stripped the bloodied white elbow-length gloves from Laura Providencia's arms, dropped the gloves in the sink, and turned on the water faucet. She did all this slowly, softly asking questions until finally Laura answered in Spanish, and Miss Hamilton seemed to grasp the gist of Laura's responses. Miss Hamilton produced a handkerchief from the sleeve of her gray tunic. She soaked the handkerchief under the running faucet.

Laura stared into the mirror above the sink and watched the old white lady with blue hair wash her face with the wet handkerchief. In slow circular motions, the old white lady restored Laura Providencia's face to brown. Laura glanced at the adjacent sink brimming with water turning red; the bloated fingers of the floating glove waved at her.

PHILIP LEVINE

Unfinished

He lived with a pack of stray dogs up in the hills
beyond Tibidabo. I went first to see the house
shaped like a flower, a late unfinished work
of the great Gaudí, and found the wild man, bearded,
dressed for winter on a hot June afternoon
in the dense pine forests: jackets over jackets,
two pairs of gray woolen pants full of moth holes.
I'd surprised him coming as I did alone on foot
the last half mile and found him brewing something
in a coffee can over a little smoking fire
in the cellar. With a long wooden staff he roused
the dogs sleeping around him. I stood speechless
while he, too, barked, in Catalan or nothing,
shaking the staff above his head and would not answer
me in Spanish. And so I left. And returned
some days later to find three uniformed boys
pelting him with pebbles. I scared them off.
Little fascists, he told me, from the summer camp
up the hill. "Their idea of fun." This day we spoke,
I standing above his cellar hole and he below,
cradling a moth-eaten brown mongrel who also
had been hit and gazing now and then up at me
to answer my questions. With his long beard gone white
and his wild voice, I had thought him ancient and mad,
some relic of the war hiding from the police
since '39. He offered to share his soup.
In one gloved hand he held up the steaming can,
in the other a wooden spoon. When I refused
he raised his dark brows and laughed. "This is home,"
he said, "I live and worship here. I welcome you."
When I returned with a sort of care package
of cheese, salami, and chocolate bars, I met him
coming up the trail to the place. "Unfinished,"

he told me, Gaudí had died alone, unknown,
like him, and the work had stopped. This time I saw
he was only my age, for in spite of one bad leg
he made his way up the hill with ease, naming
the wild flowers along the way and calling the dogs
who romped ahead. He laid a plank out for us
to cross the moat. "Careful," he said, "careful,"
as we crossed the rotting floor to where a stairway
descended to the cellar. Side by side we sat
on metal crates, and he pointed up to where
a line of white clouds rode above the few rafters
that were the roof. As a boy he'd loved houses
like this, unfinished, open, for they left
nothing out. He could play in them all day
and come back alone at night when the stars
drew near and whispered their names. "I was happy,"
he said. "I would sleep and waken in the stars."
He accepted my package with a courtly little bow
of his narrow shoulders, and we shared a slab
of white Gallegan cheese he cut in long strips
with a pocket knife. "I will skip the soup today,"
he said and laughed again. I never returned.
I never saw him again though I lived nearby
for the rest of that year and came back often.
On the way down the hill a strong wind picked up
moaning through the pines and raising the harsh dust
of the trail into my nose and mouth until
I almost choked. I doubt that was why. I don't
know why. I know that when I asked him what
happened when it rained he laughed a last time.
"Why then everything is clean. The house is clean."

Lilac

Before work I would stop by Constantine's place
for a glass of red wine and a cup of coffee.
He kept the wine under the counter and poured
it in secret into a large tumbler. "If anyone asks,"
he once said, "tell them it's the milk of a red cow."

You could tell which men were coming off the job.
Half-asleep, they slumped along the counter talking
to no one. If you asked one for a light he'd look
sideways at you as though you'd just lost your mind.
More than once I did lose my mind. I'd begin to sing

off-key in Yiddish about the joys of wine,
a tune my grandpa sang when he was young and flush
or whenever Sadie, his wife, threatened to leave.
(Grim-faced and resolute after forty years,
she left claiming she couldn't take another day.)

Always the same guy, a red-faced giant we called Mack,
would shout out without looking around, "Tell the kike
he can't carry a tune." In Constantine's "kike"
was the formal term for a Jew dumb enough
to work swing shift at Chevy Gear & Axle.

The smoke rising toward the ceiling or billowing
out the door into the winter air was lilac
in color and always made us think of spring,
of the high secret meadows, wind-blown, just below
the white peaks of the Pyrenees above Prades

or the backyard of our first house on Pingree
where the perfume of April was stronger than wine.
The evening I took the garbage out with Sadie
she warned me not to try to pet the rat, purple
in the late light, who came toward us without moving.

When without warning Constantine up and died,
an old woman in black, his mother or his wife,
came to the locked door to tell us, "No open."
Mack and I stood out in the street, snow gathering
on our shoulders, stamping and blessing the red air.

The Uses of Wine

The wine is perfect, an arterial red,
a red so serious in candlelight it's black.
He lifts the chipped glass and toasts his brother
with a slight nod, a little backward gesture
of the head only the two of them understand.
The late night crowds around the closed windows
giving back the two old men, the three candles,
the long dark table, the absence of food,
plates, silverware, napkins in the empty house,
womanless, the children long gone, the pets dead.
This never happened. You made it up because
life should end as bad books do, or so you think,
with the two antagonists facing each other
for a wordless moment clarifying everything.
He drinks his brother's health; his brother does not
drink his, for he can no longer drink at all.
I can almost hear you say, "Something is missing."
Brotherless yourself, far younger than these two,
you see the two parted by their separate lives
come together at the end while the night calms
until a distant police siren reminds
them where they are. They're home. It's perfect,
all that was lost, you say, will be found in wine,
wine that is ancient, wine that tastes of ashes.

NICK FLYNN

Embrace Noir

I go back to the scene where the two men embrace
& grapple a handgun at stomach level between them.

They jerk around the apartment like that
holding on to each other, their cheeks

almost touching. One is shirtless, the other
wears a suit, the one in the suit came in through a window

to steal documents or diamonds, it doesn't matter anymore
which, what's important is he was found

& someone pulled a gun, and now they are holding on,
awkwardly dancing through the room, upending

a table of small framed photographs. A chair
topples, Sinatra's band punches the air with horns, I

lean forward, into the screen, they are eye-to-eye,
as stiff as my brother & me when we attempt

to hug. Soon, the gun fires and the music
quiets, the camera stops tracking and they

relax, shoulders drop, their jaws go slack
& we are all suspended in that perfect moment

when no one knows who took the bullet—
the earth spins below our feet, a blanket of swallows

changes direction suddenly above us, folding
into the rafters of a barn, and the two men

no longer struggle, they simply stand in their wreckage
propped in each other's arms.

The Deliberate Mistake

I wanted the Persian Isfahan rug
with the all-over garden of paradise design,
the one with one thousand two hundred knots
per inch. Its sinister history
was of no importance to me,
irrelevant the conditions of
the weavers, whether they
were hungry or suffered from
carpal tunnel syndrome. I loved

the way the tree of life reached out
to me with its swirling tendrils,
tickled even the arches of my feet,
then, indifferent to my pleasure,
turned back again onto
some other purpose.
Better than furniture, a carpet
is for standing on. From my
five feet six inches I could

survey with majesty the
panorama of its radiance: vegetal
dyes of ochre, madder root, bark,
cochineal beetle and berries, kurk wool
from the chests of young lambs
reared in the Himalayas.
All on cotton warp and silk weft.
Colors designed to ravish:
indigo and saffron and yellows
from pomegranate skins.

And then to apprehend
the deliberate mistake.
The floral border, a camouflage
of magenta and nomadic browns,
hides the discrete flaw, a gesture
in deference to Allah's monopoly
of perfection. Wiser the risk
of a client's approval than the
alienation of a vain and selfish god.

We chose, instead, the Jaipur
rug with one knot per inch
for every humble year of the raj.
Gray, the color of secrets,
green for constancy, the hue of
Mohammed's coat, holy, proud,
assertive with desire.
Something honest in its William Morris
merino swirl attracted me. Its jute
foundation coarse and to the point.

RICHARD CECIL

Why I Have No Children

When I turned twelve and feared I'd go to hell,
I used to write lists of my mortal sins
on paper scraps I tucked into my wallet.
Each time I broke one of the big commandments—
not little ones, such as to honor parents
which even Jesus, like me the son of peasants,
had never really managed to obey—
I'd score a mark next to the sin's code name.
ITA meant Impure Thoughts and Actions,
which, I was told, were what was forbidden
by Thou Shalt Not Commit Adultery
and Thou Shalt Not Covet Thy Neighbor's Wife.
ITA got almost all my slash marks,
like the front runner in a landslide election.
Although I treaded ants and swatted flies
I never checked the "K" for "Shalt Not Kill."
And though I coveted my neighbors' goods,
such as the boy next door's Deluxe Parchisi,
I never stole, but only begged and whined
until I got the stuff I really wanted—
everything except the model airplane,
marked "$10" in the dime-store window,
which really flew, and burned real gasoline.
All year I hoarded lunch and candy money,
then, on my birthday, my rich uncle Tony
doubled my life savings with a five.
Abe Lincoln's kindly portrait seemed to say:
"You're free, boy. What you want is yours."
I waved the bill and danced a jig of joy.
And then, out of the blue, my mother said,
"That plane's dangerous. I won't let you buy it."
"Goddamn you to Hell I hate you!" I spat out
and ran up to my room and slammed my door

and barricaded it with a chest of drawers.
Even now, as I write down my curse,
I shake with rage. What I remember best
of eighteen years of living with my mother
is the one thing she wouldn't let me buy,
not even with my own hoarded money.
I dreamed, again, last night of that plane.
I laid my crisp new five and wrinkled ones
and quarters, nickels, pennies, and a dime
on McCrory's shiny counter, and the clerk
with hooks instead of hands clawed up my cash
and punched ten dollars in the register,
and everything I'd been denied was mine,
until I woke and remembered my dead mother.
This is my confession of the sin
I never marked down on my childish list.
I doubt that it will ever be forgiven.

ANN CHOI

Passion Week

for Kyo-jin

When Mrs. Im went back to Seoul to die
it rained and I thought of her dying.
It was March and cold there
though it made no difference to her
her hair no longer blue-black shoulder-length
spirals of a young Mrs. Im
the wife of Pastor Im's brother
but frizzy wire ends flattened by pillows.
I heard the rain and I thought of death.
But I knew nothing of it
and couldn't mourn
so I told my friends
someone is dying of liver cancer in Seoul
they said without thinking
we're here what can we do for you

This week you come visiting from Wellington
the curls at your temples
golden from the sun and graying.
There is no more death in you
than in mushrooms and pea pods
though your love is many persons
now inactive now suicidal
now piercing her navel and meeting
men in bars. Now I know.
So where is the passion
in wanting to have been something useful
like a shovel or an arm?

Knowledge distracts us
and makes us bad company
when it doesn't become a search for more.
How do I offer you a heart
stiffening in its cave?
It is already Friday and I
could be mourning.

Someone is dying on a tree
and all I can do is think
come down
what can you do for me
come down.

Waiting for a Bicycle

It was July
and the peaches were green

a man born
in the year of the chicken

with no knack for wealth
or common knowledge

lowered the box full of green peaches
for a girl to see

a girl at the front gate
turning eight and waiting

for a thing of wheels
this is where memory fails

did a small mouth fall
into a crate full

of fruit or did it speak
the usual greeting at dusk

falling behind the loaded
gait of a man

walking past a girl
through a yard where a house bird

pecks sometimes at grain
and sometimes stone

how blind is love
how feckless its genuine wings

Raccoon

With his two hands
   covering his two eyes
      he prays in the middle of the road

over the clump of fur and bone
   that was himself.
      He looks like my old *zayde*

in the synagogue
   two decades ago
      ashamed for his poverty.

Comedian of the hard frost,
   deft champion of screw-on tops,
      more than once we met

over the garbage of daily life—
   you poised on the proscenium
      of a metal lid,

me caught in the isosceles
   of an upstate porch light.
      For forty years my grandfather stitched

linings into women's suits
   under a searchlight the shop foreman hung
      over the old man's head.

Sometimes he slapped his son with his hat
   when he got home and cursed his boss
      for making him sew on the Sabbath.

Not even a coat will be made of you,
brother raccoon, you who did not outlive
this year's bachelor buttons and marigolds,

who secured whatever flesh
you could find and made your way
dragging your black-ringed tail

across the collaborating streets at dawn
where the local truckers
in their shiny rigs stop at nothing.

JON LOOMIS

In the Lutheran Nursing Home,
Grandma Lula Tells Two Stories

How Uncle Alvin tumbled from the hayloft,
broke his neck. How once a one-armed hobo,
a black man, split a half cord of stove wood

for a plate of ham, green beans, and fried potatoes,
which he ate, slowly, sitting on the grass
in the shade of a doomed elm tree.

Great-grandma stepped out on the porch
with a glass of buttermilk, a slice
of rhubarb pie, saw the half-starved

barn cat nosing into the hobo's dinner—
he couldn't push the cat away and eat
at the same time. Without thinking

anything, she yelled "Hey, you, Blackie—"
the cat's idiotic name, "Hey, you,
get away from there!" The hobo stood

awkwardly, still holding his plate,
gunnysack tucked under his one elbow.
He gave her a terrible look, then walked out

into the dusty road, around the bend
at Nafziger's woods and out of sight forever.
"How awful," says my mother. "The poor man."

"Three weeks later, someone burned the barn,"
Grandma sighs, poking at her applesauce.
"We had good food then. Not like this stuff."

"Did the hobo burn the barn?" my brother asks—
he's twelve. "What happened to his arm?
What did he do with the plate?" But Grandma's

gone again. She's back on the farm—fast
in her new dress, chasing the fat ducks
over the hill and down to the cool green pond.

The Speed Break

"Break a board's good as a *rib*," says my teacher,
flexing his fists, "—ain't no rib stayed in one place *that* long!"

My shoulder aches from holding my arm at eye-level. My wrist aches
forming a crook. And my fingers and thumb, too, for pinching
between them a board, the grains of which slope toward a black knot.

"Come on, man," he says, clapping his knuckles together,
"—wait there like a *statue the cat* who wouldn't *punch*."

But I do, slowly, in practice, move my free arm forward, knuckles
turning over and fist squeezing as I tap the board, withdraw
the fist, tap the board, knuckles turning over as I withdraw the fist.

"Come on, *man*," my teacher says. But I'm all stares
at the black knot. Staring, as he concludes, softly, "—*Shit*."

A scene I can't possibly imagine. The gun tapping Warren's back.
Then a twitch, then a flash. No pain, nothing but a thin mix
curling down the shoulder chunk. A hole in his back. The black knot.

My teacher takes the board, and in one swift, generous motion,
snaps it over his knee, adding, "—Something *broken*."

Toughest of breaks, the speed break. The fist must fracture the wood
by causing a whiplash, reversing as hard and fast as it strikes.
And then, to let both pieces fly from fingers and thumb, clattering . . .

My teacher stalks off, muttering, "—Time and chances."
In his hands, not just the halves, but the wound, the undoing—

A True Story

A woman visits the auto showroom down her street, carefully
    inspects all the glamorous, unattainable cars,
opens the door of an all-white Lincoln convertible and gets in.
    A salesman with sideburns walks over,
says how-do, asks her if she'd like to take it for a spin. "Sure," she
    says, and off they go around the block,
the wind gentle in her hair, the sun warm on her face, the ball of
    her foot throbbing from all that power. "Thanks," she says
as they return, and before she leaves she watches him snag the
    ignition key on a hook behind his desk.
That night, halfway through *Unsolved Mysteries,* she rises from
    her couch, pulls the fire extinguisher from its rack in the kitchen,
walks back to the showroom, and lobs it through the big plate-
    glass window. She gets the keys to the Lincoln, rams it
over the low sill in a shower of sparks, and heads for the
    SuperAmerica, where she fills the tank, picks up an armload
of Pepsi and Fritos and dip. *I don't have to pay,* she says on her
    way out. *Jehovah is my father.*
The cashier and the manager run after her, and when she tries to
    drive off, the car won't go in reverse.
They hold both doors shut to keep her in, so she puts it in park,
    stares straight ahead, keeps her hands
tight on the steering wheel, waits for the inevitable while the
    engine idles. Four cruisers pull in, lights flashing. Soon
she is handcuffed, gently eased into a back seat. On the way to
    the station she looks in the windows of many houses:
generous draperies, cheerful rooms, the blue flicker of unseen
    televisions, the parents who sit before them in faceless silhouette.

Mayo ham & cheese

mayo ham & cheese   *mayonnaise, jambon, fromage*   lettuce, tomato
two slices wheat bread   golden delicious apple   pack of snack crackers
iced tea in the fridge   (instant) or if you prefer   instant lemonade
they're feeding us too well   not that I'm getting worried   I'm enjoying camp
I think I'll come back   that's better than misery   better than despair

someone claims Braque said: *I should be utterly lost   if I knew where I*
was going; and that *If   you know where you are going   you will surely not*
get there was said by   Leonardo; that Tolstoy   said, *What you may not*
have above all in   making a novel is pre-   conception; and that
Picasso once said,   *I find first, seek afterward*   someone else says it's
Brancusi who said,   *Things are not difficult to   make; what's difficult*
is putting ourselves   in the state of mind to make   them —these give us hope—

kind of you to ask   yes, my heart's a checkerboard   with some darker parts
you have spoken well   we must be more wary now   too much is tacit
& then violent   has your lover never beat   or bit or scratched you?
let us pray for peace   that peace may descend from clouds   of full divulgence
& then when we play   no one needs to take the role   of mere dumb body

185

Satchmo

SIDE A—
the face handled
careful, black

wax grooves
going round
in an endless

endless grin—
King Louis
Armstrong

blowing like no
tomorrow.
Oooh hoo

I wanna be
like you-who—
Pops wipes his brow

with a kerchief
as if cleaning
a needle, a skipping

dusty LP.
An ape like me
would love to be

human too.
SIDE B—
his bull

horn muffled,
sounding fog—
labels spun

too fast
to read. Heebie
Jeebies. *Is*

you is or is
you ain't—
Satchelmouth

Old Scratch, caught
between the devil
& the deep

blue sea—his Hot Fives
scat, out-play
Beezlebub on a good

day—two horns
twisted
up out his hair—

In the Library of Unrecorded Lives

There's one good book in everyone, or so the saying goes,
at least one, and I like to think of Miss Shaughnessy,

my third-grade teacher, hair bunched back in a crimped bun,
dress as drab as those gray afternoons spent dreaming

in her class, eyes two magnified minnows behind glass
thick as astronomical lenses—could she have had a life?

Could she have dreamed of swashbucklers and maids,
murder and sex merging in a narrative so gripping

little boys would stop griping and fall silent under its spell?
And what of Rosa, Rosa Puckett, face pale as oatmeal,

soft sac of silence we attacked like hornets, beleagured figure
of fourth-grade fun? Could she have harbored romance,

longed behind that shabby scowl for some exotic rendezvous
on foreign sand? Or Tony Conecci, block of meat,

ham-fisted son of immigrants—could he ever have imagined
heroes with a swagger, cloak-and-dagger exploits

beyond the weekend pounding he withstood as center
on the football squad? What of their lives and so many others

God seemed loath to honor, nameless lumpen
in the pageant of my own pubescent brain? Yet here they are,

radiant in memory, each a star in the mind's
incorruptible eye: Nero Legér, flashing horse teeth

when he laughed, arms jutting out of tattered cuffs;
Peggy Hood, so shy her feet scuffed circles when she spoke,

butt of every joke we could muster, which only made her stammer
worse. What of their lives, unrecorded in any book?

I'd love to slip their volumes off the shelf and have a look,
settle in to read the wealth of life denied—learn

what Andy Washburn felt the night his ailing mother died,
who coughed up fifty years of smoke and vanished;

or Cindy Fitz, banished on a withered leg, tall as a fence post
and as lonely. Ordinary figures of disappointment and strife.

If there's one good book in everyone, I'd love to browse
those pages after years of currying my own regard.

Lucent populations of the soul: it's for you I lay down my life.

The Big Fish

It was a simple choice, the way she figured, and I still think she was right. Either she went willingly, ignoring everything still unsettled, or she could refuse and risk guilt for the rest of her life.

So there really was no choice. She made a reservation, bought a suitcase, and headed for the airport.

But you should have seen her the week before. An hour or so a day walking the streets, talking of nothing else to everyone she met.

Each of whom had the same reaction to her story that she was going to spend four days with her parents, at their home, for the first time in twenty-two years.

"You mean you haven't seen them in twenty-two years?"

"No, I have a few times, but here. We've gone out for lunch, with the children."

"Oh. Well. That will be a heavy trip." To a man, there was fear in their eyes. The women rolled theirs. One confided: "Whenever I go home, I can't sleep." Another said he lost, after three days at home, whatever adulthood he'd acquired.

So then she, for whom the sentiment of *going* home didn't exist, because she was at home where she was, nevertheless began to worry that there would be more to it. Some awful secret that would render her a child. Events she had run from and forgotten. Love aggrieved. Some home still there.

Scared, she caught a stomach flu, or maybe it was nerves. Couldn't eat for a couple of days. Got delayed packing and had to wash her hair at the last minute.

But finally she did leave, on a bright February day, in a taxi, since her father was paying. When they reached that high point on the BQE at the Kosciusko Bridge, and every building in Manhattan stood revealed along the curved horizon, she said to herself, but only once: It's a day to be coming not going.

Then she turned her eyes toward Miami.

On the plane, her appetite returned as soon as she was served.

So it *was* a bug, she thought, not some gastrointestinal response to anxiety. Relieved, she relished the bad food.

The champagne helped, too. She toasted her seatmate and told him her story. Of him, she learned that after a boyhood on the Lower East Side, he'd become a diamond merchant, traveling extensively. Now, though, he had semi-retired to Florida and got most of his exercise, he said, between the sheets. When he inquired as to the cause of this long separation from her family, she replied: It was for love. He nodded sadly. Had he had the courage to marry *his* shiksa, he said, he'd have led a far better life. Instead he'd spent twenty years with someone he detested. Lizzy pitied him, worn by his anger, and when he asked for her number and said he'd take her out sometime, she wasn't displeased. Cute in a graying way, she decided. But then he handed her an old, wrinkled card. Oh well, she thought, and then they landed.

But I forgot to say she'd been hemming a skirt, flashing her thimble all through the air over the Eastern seaboard. Another chore left undone. What had they called her at that long-ago home? Last-Minute Lizzy, she remembered.

With her head bent over this task, her wet braided hair fell across her face. She'd spent the first decade of her life with four braids in her hair, as styled by her mother, two in front "to catch the short ends," which were then braided into the back two, the effect a sort of Mediterranean Heidi. Relocated now on her own aesthetic map, she sometimes hung her front braids out.

Anyway, her hair had dried and the skirt was done when Lizzy got off the plane and descended to the luggage madness. A long wait ensued, and she knew she should call to let her parents know she'd arrived, but it was hard to drag herself away from the hope that hers would be the next suitcase round the bend. When finally she did phone, the line was busy. After a few tries, she fought her way back through the crowd, found her bag, and went for the limo. It wasn't there. The service her mother had told her to take didn't operate at that airport. The driver she did find claimed, after some discussion, that her destination was not on the map of Miami. And wasn't she herself saying she'd never been there? Even her insistence that mail got through was discounted; he seemed not to credit that at all. However, at last, despite his reservations, he consented to drive her around—all night, if necessary.

Lizzy sighed, wiped sweat, and squeezed herself into a corner of the car, feeling homesick and as though she'd crossed some border while the driver stuffed in ladies with diamonds on their arthritic fingers.

It seemed like another very long time before they started and until each of the ladies was driven within inches of her very front door and carefully, deferentially, unloaded. But eventually Lizzy found herself alone with the driver on a palm-lined road that wound between concrete castles at once large and insubstantial. "Which way is the sea?" she asked, as she'd never seen a Southern one and even a view of it in the dark seemed appealing. But when he gestured at the neon-lit motels to their left, she gave the idea up—anyway, it was already an hour since the plane had landed, and she knew her parents would be worried. She began to discuss the address once more, but in her confusion kept calling it by the name of the Cuban arts council, which was "esactly" the same "escept" for two letters. It was to her immense relief, then, that they finally turned at a sign into an underground garage. And here the *driver* began to seem nervous. Ramps, levels, numbered stalls, were everywhere, you *could* drive around all night. When he spied some people walking at the far end, he sped after them, and for a moment, frazzled as Lizzy was, she thought he would run them over.

Luckily he didn't, for they'd been placed there, it seemed, by divine chance: her parents' next-door neighbors.

And so it was that Lizzy found herself in an elevator, crowded between two elderly couples who had undertaken with pleasure to deliver her. Four storks four for this rebirth. The day's assault on her senses heightened. Each questioned her, smiled, stared, they would have turned her upside down and shook her if they could've. The hullabaloo increased when they reached her parents' apartment and crowded into the open doorway, where her father, after greeting her, began to thank her escorts, while she, shoving her bag, advanced toward her mother, who was also talking and wailing, her hands in the air in a gesture of supplication, Liz thought, but later realized that this was coupled with a lack of comprehension of why these people had brought her daughter. They spilled into the living room, reenacting the drama of their finding her in the garage and rescuing her from the infamous limousine service that charged a mint but didn't know a thing (well, the building's new, someone contended, you can't blame them, it's hard to see from the road). Then her parents, of course, played can-you-top-this. When she hadn't come—or *phoned,* they added pointedly—why, they had wanted to call the police! Why, they had *actually* called the airline, the terminal, the terminal they had called many times... And in defense, then, Lizzy felt obliged to pitch her own stories of the crowd and the busy phone into the excitement flying around the room.

But ultimately the door was shut, and she faced her mother, who in the year since Lizzy had seen her had shrunk to some impossibly small size, and who now embraced her from this inferior position, saying, "Well, now I can have a good cry." And so she stood holding her little weeping mother, as small as a twelve-year-old, and she thought, not without some regret, Here I won't be a child. But then—a step back, the critical eye, even from lower down—your hair! No good, the hair, and here her father joined them and concurred. "You look like a pi-," said her mother, "a pic-, a picka-, pic-pic-pic, picpicpic..."

Here let us leave our Lizzy freeze-frame a minute. Would her mother really say the word pickaninny, and start this visit off with a bang? Well, she might have, but she couldn't remember it until two days later, during another hair discussion, and then Lizzy herself in sarcasm said it, and her mother happily, obliviously cried out, "*That's* the word I was trying to remember!" But at this first moment, she, Lizzy, seeing in an instant what was required, wisely launched a verbal distraction, and towed them along until they were all safely drinking tea and opening the presents she had brought them.

But when, later, she lay adjoining her mother at one end of the L-shaped daybed arrangement of the bedroom (her father in the living room on the couch), the strangeness of it all assailed her. Though certainly she could manage four days, she thought, especially in the sunny South, midwinter. Still, she fell asleep thinking of the diamond man's bitter life, and not of these two old people breathing near her.

The next day was Lincoln's Birthday. There in the South you would never have guessed. Just as you would never have guessed, watching Lizzy between her mother and father, their delighted introduction of her to their friends around the pool, and the smiles exchanged under that pastel sky, that this family had no recent history.

Neither would you know, except for my telling you, that as she hemmed her skirt on the plane, Lizzy had remembered her mother pinning a hem for her, asking, "Who was that Negro boy you said hello to?"

Lizzy had long gone her separate way when her father, ill, sent for her. A few years after that, on a visit north, he met her children. In Lizzy's kitchen, he kissed their hands.

I am reminded, telling this, of an encounter she had one summer evening in a college town. She had differed, loudly and good-humoredly, with a Pole who claimed to recognize her. "There's a history of you in Europe," he said. "When we sent our girls to school with the goyim, all the smart ones married Marxists so they could leave the ghetto and change the world."

Lizzy had laughed, but she had left the ghetto on her own.

Still, now, in Miami, she began to feel guilty as they went upstairs and she helped her mother prepare the frozen food cooked in too much water. Should I have demanded more of them, she wondered, should I have insisted, *You must love us, you must let us love you!* What ought I to feel, now, that I don't? An evening of TV stupefied her. That second night, in dreams she chased an elusive man—her lover, though; not her father.

In the morning, she was up before them, and over a cup of instant coffee and what seemed to be the same piece of oilcloth on the kitchen table that she remembered from twenty-two years before, wrote in a journal: Air. Air. Air.

They lived a couple of blocks from a beach they never went to, across the way from a pool they never swam in, in an air-conditioned apartment with the air off and the windows shut. It was neat but neglected; her mother shuffled around and was forgetful; her father, his prostate troubled, had smelly pajamas.

Air, she gasped, but neither would walk with her when they woke, so she went out alone. The previous day's guilt persisted. What had she done for them in return for her life? And the question of emotion: it was too strange to feel so little.

Outside, at the elaborately landscaped entry to the building, a young man was slumped in the cab of a trailer truck. So bored, she thought, too bad. She walked on, to a place she had seen from the window, a sandy lot beside a waterway, and sat down among some intricate, wicked-looking weeds, hoping to smoke a joint and come to some conclusions. The hot sun on her back felt terrific. She shut her eyes. Almost immediately two sounds in sequence—ordinary sounds, first a hammer, then a gull—completed, with the sand and sun, a scene she had once imagined and described. Once again, life follows art, she thought, and it was with gratitude that she thought then of her father, who had made this correspondence possible. If I can feel this, I'll have other feelings, she thought, and jumped up to return to the house.

The young man was still morose in his truck. She couldn't leave him like that. "You haven't left," she said, and he said, "Nope." He came from Rhode Island, he told her. His boss was inside, trying to get a load for the trip back. He liked his job, but sometimes, like now, it was a drag. "Here," she said, as she was about to go, and left him open-mouthed, holding the joint.

So it wasn't only her thanks but this bonhomie that she carried back to her father, who was sitting in his chair—yes, *his* chair. She kissed him when she walked in, and as she went into the bedroom, she could hear, loud through his tracheotomy, a sigh of satisfaction.

That evening, with her mother, Lizzy looked at old photos. There was just one missing from the album, a proof she had asked for in letters, taken on the day she'd first fought for control: at ten, combed her hair the way *she* wanted. The proof was nowhere to be found, her mother adamant it didn't exist. They nearly argued. But then Lizzy found a picture of herself she'd never seen, taken just before she had never gone home again, a snapshot of her as a young woman, seated in front of a window, her hand extended as though reaching for something. There I was, here I am, she thought, and was content. Her mother also liked that picture. Like a girl reporter, she said, and gave it to Lizzy as a present.

The next day was Valentine's, and they went to a dance. Her father, once a terrific man on the floor, still had rhythm but was more subdued. And he wouldn't Latin. He did bum a cigarette for her, he who had lost his voice to cancer, and stood outside with Lizzy while she smoked it. After one drag, she didn't want it, but took her time because it was so clearly his remembered pleasure.

With her mother she danced also, in the lead position, twirling her around until the little woman was dizzy and then got the giggles, tears pouring out of her eyes as Lizzy steadied her and kissed her. A woman commented, "You don't usually see a daughter kissing her mother," and Lizzy, thinking of her own three, thought, That's what you don't see, lady. But her mother had made a noodle dish for the dance and then didn't want to share it. "But you must!" Lizzy cried out, astonished.

The next day it rained steadily, and she thought at first she wouldn't go out, but then decided to anyway. "In the rain?" they worried. "To get things for the children," she insisted, and found an umbrella.

But everything in the souvenir shops had been made in the Philippines. She went from store to store, until at the end of a wide boulevard she saw an open space, between two buildings, that looked as if it might be a way to the sea. Which since the night of her arrival she had purposely forgotten, in order to concentrate on wanting, for once, to be with her parents more than in the world.

Excited now, she crossed the street and ascended a slight sandy rise. And there it was, impossible *aqua marina,* a Southern sea even under such a rainy sky.

There was a fishing pier to her left, and she went to read the sign on it. Admission was fifty cents. But under the pier, she noticed, you could get right up to the water. As she stood deciding, a man came down the ramp toward her. He was carrying a bucket, and when they smiled at each other, she was pleased that the South could trick her, and that she and this black man could greet in some polite and uncomplicated manner. She asked about his catch, and he told her the names of the fish. "Well," she said, "I think I'll just go swimming instead, even if it *is* raining," and they laughed together before saying goodbye.

The pier stank of creosote and gulls, but Lizzy waded into the warm surf and picked up three little perfectly shaped shells. And then a small white sailboat appeared, moving slowly across the horizon.

And that was enough. I can remember *this,* she thought, and turned to go, anxious lest her parents worry she was gone too long in the rain, and besides she hadn't yet bought a single thing for the children.

She walked up the beach, glancing from time to time over her shoulder at the perfect little sailboat in the perfectly blue sea, until she realized it was no longer raining. As she stopped to close the umbrella, a man came toward her. She glanced at him and then past him to a small knot of people. He smiled as he went by, and noting her curiosity, pointed to the group, and said, "Beeg feesh."

Beeg feesh? She grinned at him and then approached the group, who indeed had a big fish, lying there on the sand, sleek and dead and heavy-looking. She gazed at it, dismayed, for something about its flesh was doglike, and then looking up met the eyes of the young blond woman whose fish it was, who stood over it. There was such a look in them, oh! Lizzy glanced around but met on every side the same spirit, though none so full of it, so completely hateful, it seemed, as that of the girl.

She turned away and continued walking, her good mood arrested. As if just the sight of her had been enough for them to suspect she might steal it, steal their beeg feesh. When she had only wanted to see it. She made her way back, preoccupied and without presents, but then, feeling the three little shells in her pocket, thought the children would like those, fixed up nice, because at least they were really from Miami.

So she rejoined her parents, and spent another pleasant evening saying little. In the morning, her mother waved goodbye from under the covers, accepting a kiss with her eyes half-shut.

Her father drove her to the airport. When she stood waving at him from the sidewalk in front of the terminal, he kept his eyes fixed on the road. But he was eighty and didn't drive too well anymore, and Lizzy was grateful that he'd even offered.

This time her seatmate on the plane was a lawyer, and they breakfasted chatting about children and careers. Lizzy felt relieved to have an extended conversation, as if it proved her intact.

But she was eager to be home. The weather in New York was cold and unpleasant, during the night it had snowed. She took a taxi she could ill afford, and they got stuck for half an hour on the Kosciusko, the meter jumping, the driver irate. It had been her idea to take the BQE. A car cut in front. "Damn nigger," the driver said.

"Big hit," her mother said, when she phoned that evening, "you were a big hit."

Big hit, Lizzy thought, then suddenly thought, *Big fish.* And hung up thinking this: You can fish in the past, but the only fish to see, finally, is the beeg feesh, the one we're all afraid the other guy will steal.

Ant

She was dozing on a faded Navajo blanket with the filmy shade of a maple tree drawn like a veil across her skin. Her blouse was still opened to where he'd unbuttoned it down to the sky blue of the bra she'd brought back as a souvenir from Italy.

Martin was lying just beyond the edge of the shadows thrown by her eyelashes. He had removed his shirt and spread it beneath him on the grass. It was hot, and lounging in her company seemed to intensify the light. Even the birds were drowsy. Only a single ant was working. It had him by the toe.

"Trying to tow me away," he would have called out to her but for the lassitude, and her aversion to puns. The Woman Who Hates Puns, she sometimes called herself.

With his eyes closed and the sun warm on his lids, it seemed as if he and the ant were the only creatures on the planet still awake. At first, Martin was simply amused by its efforts, but after a while he began to sense a nearly imperceptible movement across the grass. He squinted up into the high blue sky, not caring really where he was headed. It was a day for such an attitude, but then most any day spent with her could trigger a mood like that— could require it, in fact. Since he'd met her, Martin had increasingly spent his days in a trance for which he had no name. To describe this addicting state of mind, he joked that he was living in Limbo.

This was Limbo: high, heavenly-looking clouds that threw no shadow and assumed no shapes. No wind, yet a faint hiss in the trees. Sunlight faintly weighted with perfume. In Limbo, where dream ruled, siestas were mandatory. The grass slid gently beneath him without leaving a stain along his spine. Grass blades combed his hair as he went by until his hair assumed the slant of grass.

So long as it was only a single ant, Martin didn't mind. He wouldn't tolerate them marching up his body in black columns, swarming, entering his mouth, ears, nostrils, and eyes in a pulsing stream, as if he were just another corpse to clean.

It was a morbid vision, not in keeping with such a lovely day.

Even here in Limbo, Martin thought, one apparently never recovers from having had "Lonigan and the Ants" read to him as a child.

He could still remember his anticipation—a mix of excitement and terror—on those Sunday afternoons in summer when his uncle Wayne would arrive with a storybook under his arm. Uncle Wayne would come to baby-sit for little Martin while Martin's parents went out to the backyard barbecues from which they would return "pickled," as his father called it—though they looked more as if they'd been boiled—smelling of Manhattans, and laughing too easily and loudly.

"Remember," his mother would caution conspiratorially before she left, "don't ask Uncle Wayne about the war. He doesn't like to talk about it. And don't worry if he doesn't talk much at all."

As young as Martin was, it was clear to him that the baby-sitting was as much for Uncle Wayne's sake as it was for the sake of Martin's parents or himself.

Uncle Wayne usually didn't talk much when his parents were there. He seemed shy, embarrassed, almost ashamed. His face was pitted from acne, which gave him the look of a teenager. Sometimes, Martin imagined that Uncle Wayne's face had been pitted by shrapnel.

"Do you like stories?" his uncle had asked him during their first visit.

"Sure," Martin said.

"Good. Stories are what kept me sane," Uncle Wayne said, then laughed in the odd, stifled way of his as if at a private joke between them.

But reading aloud, his uncle lost his shyness. Uncle Wayne didn't simply read stories, he brought them to life. During "The Most Dangerous Game," Martin had to run from room to room while his uncle, reading aloud the entire time, stalked him, the storybook in one hand, and in the other a bow made from a clothes hanger strung with a rubber band and armed with an arrow fashioned from a cardboard pant guard.

When they read "The Monkey's Paw," Martin hid behind his bedroom door while his uncle mounted the stairs with the heavy-footed, ominous tread of someone dead who'd been summoned back from the grave. Nearly quaking with fear, Martin had tried to wish him back into his grave while his uncle Wayne pounded on the door.

His uncle would open the book by Edgar Allan Poe and turn to his favorite story, "The Tell-Tale Heart," and the boy would force himself to watch his uncle's face so as not to miss the instantaneous transformation when his uncle's eyes assumed a maniacal gleam and his mouth twisted into a malevolent smile as he read the opening words—"I'm not really mad"—then burst into a spit-flecked spasm of psychopathic laughter.

But of all the stories they read together, it was "Lonigan and the Ants" that was the most frightening and memorable. How many Sunday afternoons, while other boys watched double-headers or shot baskets at a hoop suspended above a carport, had Martin sat sweating and listening intently as Uncle Wayne read about Lonigan making his way through the jungle, evading the hordes of army ants?

The ants streamed past barriers of water and fire, relentlessly consuming everything in their path with their black grinding mandibles, mandibles that could strip a man down to his bones as neatly and savagely as a school of piranhas.

Martin ran from the ants through the house, pursued by his uncle, who was draped in a blanket that served as the amorphous shape of massing ants. Martin would race around the table with the ants gaining on him, knocking over chairs as they went. He'd gallop up the stairs with the ants at his heels, slam himself into his room, but the weight of the ants would force open the door. He'd jump on his bed with nowhere else to run or hide as the ants oozed over his feet and began to engulf him while flushed and wild he'd beat at them with a pillow, tussling, wrestling, and finally, overpowered, nearly smothered by them, he'd have to scream, "Lonigan doesn't die! The ants don't get him! The ants don't win!"

Only then, reminded of the authority of the story, would his uncle sink back, his acne feverish, hands shaking, and silently they'd both return downstairs, which is where Martin's parents would find them, eating popsicles and watching the ballgame, when they'd return home.

Remembering his uncle, Martin had forgotten the ant. There was an obvious bad pun there at which The Woman Who Hates

Puns would have groaned. But even had Martin said it aloud, she might not have heard him, for the ant had managed to work its way beneath Martin's back and, seizing his belt with its mandibles, had succeeded in lifting him off the ground the merest fraction of a millimeter, balancing Martin so perfectly that neither his head nor heels dragged. And having succeeded in carrying Martin across the boundary of Limbo, back into the ordinary world, the ant now proceeded at a considerably more determined pace.

They went along like that, hurrying away from his slumbering Love, like a grain of rice from a wedding.

ABOUT HOWARD NORMAN

A Profile by Margaritte Huppért and Don Lee

More than a few people have assumed that Howard Norman is a Canadian writer. It's no wonder, considering that most of his work—including his first two novels, *The Northern Lights* and *The Bird Artist*, both of which were nominated for the National Book Award—is set in Canada. In fact, Norman was born in Toledo, Ohio, in 1949 to Russian-Polish-Jewish parents, and he went to elementary school in Grand Rapids, Michigan.

What led him north to Canada? "As a kid," Norman says, "I spent a lot of time in bookmobiles and libraries. I went to four different elementary schools. Libraries were the one continuity. And from early on, through books, I projected a life—I daydreamed north. This is makeshift psychologizing, but perhaps part of it was that such open, vast spaces, such a sense of mystery and severe, compelling landscapes, served to counteract the claustrophobia of an inwardly collapsing home life." His father was rarely home (when he died in 1996, Norman had not seen him in twenty years). His mother secretly cared for other children to make ends meet, which Norman did not discover until he spotted her in a photo, pushing a stroller, in a friend's family album. His three brothers provided no solace, and Norman has remained estranged from two of them. His one source of warmth and refuge was his best friend, Paul, and Paul's family. But then Paul got sick all of a sudden. Two days later, he was dead from a rare blood disease.

Eventually, Norman dropped out of high school and moved in with friends outside of Toronto. One summer, he went to Manitoba to work on a fire crew, which was mostly made up of Cree Indians, and he was fascinated by their culture, their stories and folktales in particular. Norman devised a plan for his life. He decided he would write about the wilds of Canada and its tribes. During the next sixteen years, true to his word, he would live and work for extended periods in Canada and beyond, in Hudson's Bay and Greenland and Newfoundland.

Toward that end, he received his high school equivalency and studied zoology and English at Western Michigan University, where he met Stuart Dybek. He also worked at the Athena Book Store in Kalamazoo, an old-fashioned basement store crammed with books. The owners, Bernie and Dale Johnson, were Norman's closest friends, and the store was the center of his life; it was there that he found a role model in the naturalist and bird artist Edward Lear. Indeed, Norman developed an obsession with bird art. "Every extra dollar I earned went into a print by Catesby or one of Edward Lear's parrots—I remember reading Dostoyevsky's *The Gambler,* and in a sense recognizing myself. Finally, I kept a few of my favorite works, and sold the rest."

Norman left Michigan briefly for some graduate work at the Folklore Institute of Indiana University, then was offered a three-year fellowship at the University of Michigan, where he was able to focus on his translations. He had a knack for picking up Algonquin and Eskimo dialects—he's fluent in three and passable in two, a facility that curiously does not extend to any other languages, such as French or Spanish—and he concentrated on translating Native American poems and folktales. "Through correspondence I had particular encouragement in that work from W. S. Merwin and Jerry Rothenberg; I have wonderful long letters from Merwin, from his first years in Hawaii—he was very direct in his encouraging of a writing life. And the splendid translator of Chinese travel diaries, Li Chi, was in Ann Arbor then, and she was tremendously generous with her time."

In 1978, Norman put together a collection, *The Wishing Bone Cycle: Narrative Poems of the Swampy Cree Indians* (Stonehill), and for it, he was named the co-winner of the Harold Morton Landon Translation Award by the Academy of American Poets, splitting the prize with Galway Kinnell for his translations of François Villon. (To this day, Norman shares his royalties and other honoraria with the Cree community.) Still, he continued his itinerant life as a freelancer, taking on any writing assignment that came his way. He wrote field reports for journals and museums, radio plays, narratives for documentaries, ethnographic studies, children's books, and travel articles, and he worked as an interpreter and a translator for various institutions, including the World Society for the Protection of Animals. He was constantly on the move. "Deep down, I think I still harbored some hope of

Sigrid Estrada

constructing a life somewhat like my hero at the time, Edward Lear. He was a rather eccentric traveler, and of course a wonderful artist. His travel diaries are at times painfully revealing, intimate documents of a unique man. Anyway, I had this notion of reporting back from remote places and including my sketches and drawings. An utterly autonomous life. The central failure in my thinking was that I simply could not draw."

All of Norman's far-flung work did, however, serve as a kind of literary apprenticeship. "This is difficult to articulate," he says, "since it didn't involve individual mentors as much as being steeped in—and influenced by—very different cultural traditions than my own and, of course, the centrality of oral literature to those cultures. I listened to, recorded, kept notebooks on hundreds of stories. Sometimes under formal circumstances, most often not. And even if you are slow to grasp the true emotional and historical dimensions and generosities of these myths and folktales, still, a lot of it sinks in. The structures, the rhythms, the wild episodes, the sheer inventiveness and unpredictability of incident. Of course, as a Westerner—an outsider—one can't ever think in those languages. But you can work at it. I was dogged, if nothing else. One project, transcription and translation of just

ten shaman stories from around Hudson's Bay, is just now getting
completed almost to my satisfaction, after twenty or so years.
That's pretty much how it has gone for me. Translation was a
good education. Sitting at family tables in locales such as
Churchill or Eskimo Point, filling notebooks, botching it, botching it, getting a little right. It wasn't romantic; it was just hands-
on. And it made life worthwhile for me. I think about translation
a lot. I like what Walter Benjamin said: 'A real translation is transparent, it does not cover the original, does not block its light, but
allows the pure language, as though reinforced by its own medi-
um, to shine upon the original all the more fully.'"

Yet the transient life began to wear on Norman. "I was somewhat lost, really. I knew what I no longer wanted to do: work
exclusively in remote places. But I was in kind of an agitated state.
I turned thirty. I was drinking twenty cups of coffee a day. Cafés.
Not much writing. Except that I started taking notes for a novel."
Then, in 1981, the poet Philip Levine and his wife, Fran, invited
him to Thanksgiving dinner and introduced him to another poet,
Jane Shore. "I'd been very ill with pneumonia, and was staying
out at Peter Matthiessen's house on Long Island while Peter and
Maria were in Mexico, and Franny kept phoning, saying, 'Try and
come for dinner.' And I'm glad I did; it was the most important
day of my life, meeting Jane."

It was Shore who goaded Norman into working on his fiction.
"I mean, she wanted me to be doing *something*. Jane had been
writing seriously and with total commitment since college.
Utterly dedicated to writing poetry and to teaching. I saw that
every day. And we had a talk. On one level, it was, 'Well, what do
you really want most to write?' But on a more important level, it
was, 'Why should I approve of you not trying to write the novel
you claim you want to write?' Shortly after that, Gail Mazur
asked for something for her issue of *Ploughshares*. I gave her some
pages from *The Northern Lights*—a beginning—and, bless her
heart, she took them." With the help of a Whiting Writer's Award,
he was able to complete *The Northern Lights,* in which Norman's
childhood friend, Paul, shows up as the character Pelly Bay.
"That's the one completely autobiographically-based character
I've ever written," Norman says.

Between the book's publication in 1987 and the release of his second novel, *The Bird Artist,* in 1994, Norman and Shore moved some ten or eleven times, shuttling between Vermont, Cambridge, Oahu, and New Jersey. Their daughter, Emma, was born in Honolulu in 1988 while Shore was writer-in-residence at the University of Hawaii. That same year, they bought a one-hundred-fifty-year-old farmhouse in Vermont, then promptly packed up and left. "Jane had a fellowship at Princeton, and I began teaching at the University of Maryland. New baby. New house. Employment in different places. It was like the cover of *Psychology Today:* 'Need Some Time in a Quiet Place?' "

Despite the distractions, Norman was able to publish a collection of stories, *Kiss in the Hotel Joseph Conrad and Other Stories* (Summit), in 1989; another book of translations, *Northern Tales: Traditional Stories of Eskimo and Indian Peoples* (Pantheon), in 1994; and, later that same year, his breakthrough novel, *The Bird Artist,* which had been acquired by Jonathan Galassi at Farrar, Straus & Giroux. The book was called "one of the most perfect and original novels that I have read in years" by Richard Eder of *The Los Angeles Times.* It was named one of *Time Magazine's* Best Five Books of 1994, won the New England Booksellers Association Prize in Fiction, and helped him land a Lannan Literary Award.

Norman had actually started taking notes for *The Bird Artist* more than a decade before, in 1980. "I was researching a documentary film in a fishing village in Newfoundland," he says. "I was put up in a church annex, and in that rather spartan room was a lovely watercolor of an ibis wading in the shallows. It was really a very accomplished watercolor. It was unsigned. But at the lower right-hand corner was the date, 1911. I wondered who had painted this ibis, a man or woman, and what must it have been like to have had that particular talent in that particular time and place. Who would know it? How would it be appreciated? I asked around, and found out that the artist was a young man who had been charged with murdering a lighthouse keeper. It was by and large a sordid tale, involving his mother, his half-sister, the lighthouse keeper. He was finally acquitted and went on living for years in his home village, sort of an outcast, but tolerated. He actually published three bird drawings in journals. I own one original. He died in St. Johns, Newfoundland. Anyway, I stopped researching when what I was finding out—facts—began to trespass on what I *imagined* might have taken place."

For Norman, the process of developing fictional characters has always been "an intense act of vicariousness of unpredictable duration. I think it's accurate to say, that, yes, male or female, I'd like to *be* the characters I write. Maybe not permanently—obviously not. But for the duration of the novel, yes, I would like to be those characters in those exact circumstances. To some extent, then, I invent characters out of the longing to be someone else."

This is not to say, however, that Norman is dissatisfied with his present life. Far, far from it. He has a family, a sense of belonging, that he had yearned for as a boy, and they happily divide their time between Vermont and Washington, D.C. He continues to teach one semester a year at the University of Maryland's M.F.A. program, where he is surrounded by "good students, good colleagues." Recently, he completed a collection of translations of Inuit folktales, *The Girl Who Dreamed Only Geese,* and in August of 1998, Farrar, Straus & Giroux will be bringing out his third novel, *The Museum Guard,* which Norman regards as a departure. "In the past, I'd pretty much tended to write about open spaces, how wilderness and isolation affected character, and so on. But in *The Museum Guard,* the attempt is something different. I still work with characters very 'recognizably' born out of my fictional sensibility. But this novel resides largely in interior spaces. Museums, hotel rooms, hotel lobbies. And the larger 'backdrop,' if you will, is Europe—across the ocean—and the war building up. History is imported into Maritime Canada in the form of radio broadcasts and Dutch paintings sent to a small museum in Nova Scotia, where an uncle and nephew are the only two museum guards. They are both suffering various forms of unrequited love toward the same woman, Imogen Linny, who is caretaker of the small Jewish cemetery. A painting, *Jewess on a Street in Amsterdam,* arrives at the museum, and changes their lives."

These days, it is unlikely that Norman will spend much time farther north than Vermont, where he hopes to live year-round someday, but his old journeys to the frozen climes, isolated as they were, still elicit an allegiance. "I once heard someone say, 'I'm going south to Canada.' I liked that sentence a lot."

Margaritte Huppért is a freelance journalist who often writes about American and Canadian authors. She lives and works in Montreal and Paris.

ABOUT JANE SHORE

A Profile by Lorrie Goldensohn

It was a scraggy landscape, a Vermont mentally and physically full of uneven footholds, dirt paths, and dark trees—but green with possibility. In 1965, Jane Shore and a few other classmates came to the door of Cate Farm, the place we rented from Goddard College, where my husband taught, and they all stepped in for what Jane later called my "killer spaghetti," a dish of caloric mega-tonnage that dropped the strongest. But Jane survived to become like another member of the household. Of course she was memorable: an eighteen-year-old with a bright, pretty face, a deft tongue, and a nice ringing soprano laugh.

Along with Norman Dubie, another poetry student, she was my kids' favorite baby-sitter. Once when we were ambushed by a blizzard on our way home to Cate Farm and Jane was left alone with the children for an unplanned overnight, my nine-year-old son taught her how to roast a chicken, and, in turn, she taught my eight-year-old daughter how to iron hair—put your head on the ironing board, spread your hair, turn the iron down to *Rayon*, and press flat. Jane told them stories about growing up over her parents' store in New Jersey, and somehow we all entered the life that rose so quickly into poems, poems that sparked in so many different directions that it was hard to tell where the future writing might go, but immensely easy to see that it would. From the beginning, Jane had a secure sense that making poems would be her work.

And work is the operative word, in a place and era which frankly discouraged the industrious, and where complete concentration on the weight to be accorded a word, a phrase—the sequencing of any artful raid on the immortal—was a mental practice that most people in the progressive sixties would have traded in for spontaneity alone. It's interesting that at Goddard, that home of Wild Abandon, dusted with marijuana and the call of the Impulse, Jane Shore taught herself that poetry needed craft and formal cunning, as well as the blade of feeling.

There was a sharp playfulness to her early poems, a sense of lives and styles being tried out and examined for soundness, utility. Jane was checking out the tradition in the classroom, and all the while reading and memorizing contemporary poetry in great gulps elsewhere. In addition to the Yeats and Eliot we were feeding her, she'd bring us her latest acquisition, Adrienne Rich's *Snapshots of a Daughter-in-law,* or Donald Finkel's *A Joyful Noise,* or *Somewhere Among Us a Stone Is Taking Notes,* a new chapbook by Charles Simic that she'd found at Grolier's in Cambridge, testing these things on us, forcing us to open our own eyes, think about our allegiances, and, always, working fiercely at her own poems.

Then and now, people around Jane write poetry. Then, she would bring her poems over the fields to Cate Farm, or go knock on Norman Dubie's, or Roger Weingarten's, or David Mamet's door at two in the morning, and read somebody the latest manuscript, getting and giving in return a friendly, but raking critique.

Within weeks of Jane's arrival at Goddard, word passed about Allen Ginsberg at Dartmouth. In the middle of a poetry reading, he had declared Hanover, New Hampshire, to be the "spiritual center of the universe," and dropped his pants. By the time Ginsberg made it to Goddard to read his poems, says Jane, "We were all very excited when he reached the climactic line where Plainfield, Vermont, became the spiritual center of the universe, and then we waited; but this time he didn't pull his pants down, and we were very disappointed." Very shyly, when her idol Robert Lowell read nearby, Jane invited him to come to her college. "Goddard?" Lowell answered, rearing up to his full height. "What's that?"

But it was always clear to Jane that poetry, written in solitude, is still an act of live community making, community in the widest sense: the personae in even the first of her poems stretched in time from the soldier poet Archilochus, halted in an archaic olive grove, to a future vision of herself, wheeling a shopping cart in some suburban community. If the mind proceeds from the meat of a distinct self, if you are Jane Shore, that self is always part comedienne, part chameleon, and alert, wise, curious, and acquisitive. George Starbuck, introducing her in *Lying Down in the Olive Press,* the chapbook she published at twenty-one, said: "Jane Shore knows us, gets us, talks of us or hears us talk of our-

Harry Jaffe

selves, with a faultless, unsettling, illuminating *interest*. And of herself.... [I]t's a good voice and good judgment. Not only, not even mainly, in the comic vignettes, there's the *joy* of precise observation." And this is still right.

After graduating from Goddard, Jane moved from Vermont to the Writers' Workshop at Iowa, then won a Bunting Institute Fellowship at Radcliffe, which she followed with a Briggs Copeland Lectureship at Harvard. After that, she went on to New York, Princeton, and Washington, D.C., through Guggenheim, Hodder, and NEA fellowships, and produced three books of poetry. As each appeared, the literary world tipped its hat in recognition. The first, *Eye Level,* the University of Massachusetts Press published in 1977 as the winner of the Juniper Prize. The second, *The Minute Hand*—with its eerie, unsettling cover painting of an old-fashioned child in lace collar and pantaloons, all large, anxious eyes and tight, quivering mouth, her legs folded and crossed under her rocking chair, her preternaturally delicate hands fingering an indistinguishable object—showed exactly the cross of domestic and uncanny that brought the book the Lamont Poetry Prize for 1986. The current book, *Music Minus One,* really a vividly compressed *Bildungsroman* in poems, was a finalist for the

National Book Critics Circle Award. All of these collections show the same brilliant finish, the same unerring, targeting metaphor. The folding intricacy of reference in a poem like "The Russian Doll" seems quintessential:

> at last, the two littlest dolls,
> too wobbly to stand upright,
> are cradled in her cavity as if waiting to be born.
> Like two dried beans, they rattle inside her,
> twin faces painted in cruder detail,
> bearing the family resemblance
> and the same unmistakable design.
>
> The line of succession stops here.
> I can pluck them from her belly like a surgeon,
> thus making the choice between fullness
> and emptiness;

Gentle and unstoppable, the poem advances over and through the contours of an object recognizable but exotic, graphing curve by curve the magnetic field of the nesting dolls and the perplexing pull of the generational ties between mothers and daughters, as the poem teases out the rich problematic of femaleness and female connection. Other poems into the nineties explore Jewishness and family history with the same nuanced complexity.

Eye Level occupied itself with the underside of the flesh's miracles: the flesh transforming, its boundaries eroded by loss and love. In these poems, blind albino fish adapt to an underground cavern; her father's movie camera stops and rewinds the trapeze artist's fatal fall, so that the body flies upward, instead of downward into the corpse that it became; Houdini in chains goes under the river and undoes all of his locks again. Tactile image by image, Ghiberti's doors in Florence swing open for Jane Shore backwards in time into biblical epic. Flesh is magical, clowning; and *materia,* never simply matter, streaks into the mystical.

When Jane Shore met Elizabeth Bishop at Harvard during the seventies, the older artist confirmed the odd and original angle at which the younger poet met the world and its artifacts. But like Bishop's, Jane Shore's later poems bloom overtly into dramatic narrative, grasping with an almost blind but instinctive trust for the smallest tentacle of memory, to haul forward from past time the whole huge load from which we reconstruct a life and a meaning. *The Minute Hand* spun object after object into exquisite parables of relation; but in *Music Minus One,* the pairs and things assume a new kind of *gravitas.* Shore's novelist husband, Howard Norman, pressed her to recognize the autobiographical world-scape unfolding in these poems. Jane Shore herself said of the collection as it emerged: "There was a template in my head for this book. I'd write an early childhood poem and there'd be another poem that would balance it, or fill in about a later part of my life. It was an arc, and there were points along this arc that needed to be told."

The new poetry is propelled by an urgency both formal and emotional, the world it holds peopled by her parents, her husband, and her daughter, Emma; work takes place in an old farmhouse ten minutes down the road from Goddard. As she scans her world—archaeologist of feeling, custodian of memory—the woman in Jane Shore tests the shapes of mother, lover, and daughter. While we watch in suspense—funny or painful, and so often both—she's always a virtuoso of the act, locked and shining on the trapeze bar of the poem, within those entangling alliances from which we dare not, may not, loosen ourselves.

Lorrie Goldensohn has published two poetry collections, The Tether *and* Dreamwork. *She is also the author of* Elizabeth Bishop: The Biography of a Poetry.

BOOKSHELF

APOLOGY FOR WANT *Poems by Mary Jo Bang. Middlebury College, $25.00 cloth, $11.95 paper. Reviewed by Susan Conley.*

There is quiet anarchy in the spare poems of Mary Jo Bang's haunting first collection, *Apology for Want*. The terrain is decidedly American and familiar—one of shopping malls and consumption in the "flinty age of materialism" ("The Desert on Hand"). But the voice is subversive and unsettling, the syntax wholly unique and invented for the dark, ephemeral region of longing this book inhabits.

In *Apology for Want,* desire is all-consuming. Again and again we want to possess "what is ours, the graffiti / we know: *Nut House, Weasel, Chucky Love*" ("Waking in Antibes"). With such appetite, we cannot escape the carnal, nor the hankering for the bone. In the title poem, the die is cast: "Want appropriates us, / sends us out dressed in ragged tulle." We're junkies, these poems purport—just like the heroin addict we watch "push a needle's beveled edge / into the bend of her arm, *antecubital fossa,* / / injecting the balm of habit and hit..." ("The First Room Is a Woman").

With a cool, distanced eye, Bang explores how desire humbles us, fills our waking, and presses on our sleep—eventually leading us to offer apologies. But there is no use, Bang argues: even in our highly technological age, when "...Soon we will understand everything: / why our first breath, when our last... There are few ways / to free the body from desire..." ("Apology for Want").

What I marvel here most is Bang's economy. She's a poet of stealth and answers Marianne Moore's challenge to get in and out of the poem as quickly as possible, while the poking iron is still hot. Bang writes such an immaculate line—so fierce and ardent— one is compelled to take notice, to move closer when she whispers: "It's safe to speak here. / To call love by a name other than vengeance" ("Electra Dreams").

How refreshing to read a poet inhabiting the realm of pathos who does not venture into self-pity or inflated song. These poems often clip themselves, just as they gain speed and begin to spread out. They leave us slightly stunned each time by their impact and exactitude—daring to ask the very largest of questions: "Why indelible hunger? Why insatiable need?" ("No Talking").

There is melancholia here but not mourning. Bang's unfettered "I" is not interested in self-indulgence—instead the view is more encompassing. At turns the poems are surreal and elliptical: "Once on a back yard swing / I became the sky I meant to be" ("In St. John's Hospital"). But there is also a constant assessment taking place—a vigilant addition and subtraction of our secrets and failures of the heart. Bang tries to pin desire into corners, naming and renaming it as "the shrouded want to cheek and shoulder / that arms can't reach, throat refuses to ask…"("In This Business of Touch and Be Touched").

The voice is resilient: "…Survival lies in resisting, / in the undersides of the leafed and delicate" ("Apology for Want"). Near the end of the book, Bang points to a plausible if compromised way to endure: "…where house, where dog / where a thin layer of glitter / covers years of shamed wear / and loss is now what you live with" ("Like Spiders, Step by Step"). The poems largely succeed on the strength of their anti-romanticism and in their confidence in probing the unknowable. They reveal themselves as dire warnings, which we receive thankful Bang dared put them to language.

UNRAVELLING *A novel by Elizabeth Graver. Hyperion, $22.95 cloth. Reviewed by Caroline Langston.*

In Elizabeth Graver's quietly enchanting first novel, *Unravelling,* the longings of the young narrator, Aimee Slater, are strikingly vivid and contemporary, yet the story is set in nineteenth-century New England, at the juncture between the region's rural, puritanical past and all the glittering possibilities of its burgeoning industrialization.

Beginning with her exotic name—picked by her mother from a magazine called *The Ladies' Pearl*—Aimee Slater is different from her other siblings on the farm and the other young girls of her little New Hampshire town. Born in 1829, she is headstrong and intelligent, and as she enters puberty, she is bored with the narrow opportunities offered her of housewifery and teaching; at the same time, she is pulled by a sexual desire that her mother tries by example and ominous admonition to repress. After a sexual encounter with her younger brother, an experience for which she has no language beside guilt to help her understand it, Aimee feels even further alienated from her mother and family, and from the brother who will no longer even speak to her.

Soon, however, the possibility of escape presents itself when Aimee learns of "Lowell, Massachusetts, the City of Spindles—brick building after brick building, the flowers in their window boxes, the girls coming home after work by the canal, arm in arm." Aimee is seduced by Lowell's bright utopian promises of "education in a trade" and "sewing circles and learning circles," but most of all by the prospect of independence. When an agent who recruits girls for one of the mills takes a liking to Aimee, she's not so much attracted by the future as by wanting "to see that agent watching me again," and after a struggle with her parents, she heads off for her new life.

But of course, Aimee finds life in Lowell less than utopian, with its regimented hours and slave-like mechanical labor, of which the novel is a careful document. In Lowell as well, Aimee's desires for love and physical affection culminate in her involvement with a young man, William, who at first appears ideal. Graver contrasts perfectly Aimee's characteristic need for the security he provides—"I wanted to lie down inside his coat on the floor and sleep"—to the nuances of her youthful passion, which Graver masterfully captures in lyrical language and specific detailing: "I looked down to see his hands covered with powdered sugar and pictured myself leaning over his hand, tasting the crannies between his fingers."

Ultimately, though, Aimee's awakening proves a disaster when she becomes pregnant and William refuses to marry her. She loses her baby twins to an adoption that her mother has arranged, and after returning to New Hampshire, she becomes a hermit in a hunting cabin, struggling to understand the circumstances that have brought her there. In time, she learns to recover through her own resources, and the love that has eluded her finally arrives in the person of the "town cripple" Amos; she literally stumbles over him in the forest and, significantly, helps him to clean his wounds. Through Amos, Aimee is able to resolve both the conflicts in herself and with her family. In Graver's gentle hands, these timeless, familiar themes sparkle with authenticity and poignancy.

Caroline Langston's stories have appeared in The Gettysburg Review, Ploughshares, The Pushcart Prize, New Stories from the South, *and elsewhere. She teaches literature at Rose Hill College.*

OTHER PEOPLE'S TROUBLES *Poems by Jason Sommer. Univ. of Chicago Press, $12.95 paper. Reviewed by H. L. Hix.*

Although the jacket copy on Jason Sommer's *Other People's Troubles* calls attention to the poems' focus on the Holocaust, the poems themselves wisely do not. If the jacket *shouts* Holocaust, the poems *breathe* it with the same combination of urgency and patience that must have been audible on still nights in the bunks of Buchenwald and Birkenau.

Princess Di's recent death testifies to how quickly quantity of discourse anesthetizes us to tragedy. By the third day, who wouldn't flip to *Frasier* rather than endure another news special in praise of the Princess? A similar circumstance haunts Holocaust literature. Certainly our Cynthia Ozicks and Elie Wiesels are important, but after half a dozen, who needs another? So much speech has dulled the Holocaust into a counter, a stimulus to which the response is a satisfying sorrow soothed by safe distance and a layer of dust.

Against this background, a body of poems that begins in the Holocaust can be saved from self-indulgence only by becoming essential as breath. The experiences of Holocaust victims were horrific, as were the consequences for their kin, but to explain those experiences or communicate those consequences calls for an edifice tightly masoned as *Oedipus*, language as lush as *Lear*. If even the camp guards who created and daily observed those experiences could not *see* them, we who were not there but who have heard the stories before will understand them only as other people's troubles unless finely whetted language grafts others' lives into our own.

Just such fruitful surgery does Jason Sommer perform in his evocative, funny, sad, and damn near perfect new book. "Some distance in," he begins, "a life fills / with people, / despite the early departures," like childhood friends and "the very old / who were at the gatherings once / or twice, tenderly served and seated / to the side, speaking / their other language sparingly / among themselves." Sommer's interest lies in the fact that "of those who vanish forever / you may keep a likeness," and he offers in this book a series of memorable likenesses. Meyer Tsits, for example, "the village idiot of a Munkács neighborhood," whose death ("in 1940 they practiced Holocaust / on his sort just to get the knack") was presaged by the neighborhood children making fun of him, a reminder to Sommer that "before the astounding / cruelties are the ordinary ones."

Some of the likenesses are of just such ordinary cruelties: the friend "for whom I'd written / / a letter of recommendation" who in rush-hour traffic blares her horn and shouts obscenities at the narrator apparently without recognizing him, "tailgating dangerously" in the "rage that can make strangers / / out of anyone." The focal likeness, though, is Sommer's aunt Lilly, a survivor of astounding cruelties, to whom he addresses his portrait of Mengele shitting past a hair ball in his colon grown from chewed-off bits of his own mustache. Sommer offers Mengele's unhappiness as a consolation: "a small hell in the body, such as the innocent also experience, / and that hand, which motioned thousands toward death, / those fingers reaching up his ass for years, / this thing I tell you that few people know."

The book's title poem retells a Jewish parable about "the waiting room / where all souls come," leaving each its bundle of troubles hung outside, to be picked up after its interview. As in the parable, so in the encounter with Jason Sommer's subtle and sagacious book: a soul emerges from its interview surrounded by other people's troubles, and better able to bear its own.

H. L. Hix's most recent book is Understanding W. S. Merwin *(South Carolina, 1997). His first book of poems,* Perfect Hell, *won the Peregrine Smith Poetry award and was published in 1996 by Gibbs Smith.*

PILGRIMS *Stories by Elizabeth Gilbert. Houghton Mifflin, $22.00 cloth. Reviewed by Don Lee.*

Two things are certain in Elizabeth Gilbert's first collection, *Pilgrims:* her characters possess minds of their own, and they can talk. Oh, can they talk. Gilbert is adept enough with one-line zingers ("He's too dumb to bat both his eyes at the same time"), but where she really shows her facility for dialogue is when the conversation is prolonged—people lazily teasing each other beside a campfire or in a barroom, slightly addled by drink or love, never indulging in self-pity, but simply enjoying small moments of community.

In the title story, Buck is baited by a newly hired ranchhand, a nineteen-year-old woman from Pennsylvania named Martha Knox. At first, Buck thinks he has the upper hand on her—he goes to a tree to relieve himself and says, "Shield your eyes, Martha Knox, I'm about to unleash the biggest thing in the Wyoming Rockies"—but she soon plies him with little anecdotes, dropping sinister references to her father, until Buck asks breathlessly, "You didn't kill him, did you?" Martha Knox sits down and pats his leg: "She sighed. 'Buck,' she said. 'Honey.' . . . 'You are the most gullible man I know on this planet.'"

This resistance to melodrama is the essence of Gilbert's craft. Not much happens in the book's twelve stories, despite ample opportunities, and initially it seems that the lack of action or even epiphany, the absence of propulsion in events, is a flaw. Yet, collectively, the stories build up a gentle seduction, primarily because the characters are appealing—witty, laconic, irreverent, and refreshingly uncynical.

One story states: "As an adult, Denny Brown would look back on his sixteenth summer and think that it was a wonder he was even allowed to leave his house. He would realize how woefully uninformed he was, how woefully unprepared." This could be said of the majority of Gilbert's characters—young or old, male or female, redneck or urbanite—and the fact that, naïve as they sometimes are, they don't meet catastrophe at every turn, then live thereafter in better regret, illuminates Gilbert's playful and forgiving vision of human nature.

In "The Finest Wife," Rose, a beauty pageant winner from South Texas, has, to say the least, a somewhat promiscuous past: "She had developed a bit of a taste for certain types of tall, smiling local men in dark hats. Also, she had developed a taste for certain types of church-going men and also for left-handed men, and for servicemen, fishermen, postmen, assemblymen, firemen, highwaymen, elevator repairmen, and the Mexican busboys at the restaurant where she worked (who reverently called her La Rubia—the Blond—as if she were a notorious bandit or a cardsharp)." But

Rose ends up happily married for forty-three years, and now, in her seventies, she is a kindergarten school bus driver. Only, one day, children do not appear on her route, all her former lovers do, and they climb aboard, joking, convivial, and appreciative.

The pilgrimages in this collection are remarkably varied, from a porter campaigning for the presidency of the local Teamsters union at a produce market in the Bronx to a Hungarian immigrant buying a supper club that features magic acts in Pittsburgh, but the manner in which Gilbert's characters accept their fates is surprising and charming. Even when they are about to lose their livelihood, like Ellen in "Tall Folks," when a strip club opens across the street from her tavern, meaning the sure demise of her business, there is room for celebration. She gets drunk with her young nephew, and she reminisces: "On the best nights, Ellen used to dance on that same bar with her arms spread open wide, saying, 'My people! My people!' while the men crowded at her feet like dogs or students. They used to beg her not to close. It would be daylight and they would still be coming in from across the street, begging her not to close."

EDITORS' SHELF

*Books Recommended by
Our Advisory Editors*

Maxine Kumin recommends *Black Drum,* poems by Enid Shomer: "Dazzling work by a Florida poet now living in Manhattan; Shomer weaves her net so skillfully that the reader is caught up in the story long before realizing the formal element that holds the squares in place. This book deserves serious attention." (Arkansas)

Thomas Lux recommends *Spare Change,* poems by Kevin Pilkington: "Tough, quirky, lucid poems by a poet unafraid of being understood." (La Jolla Poets)

James Alan McPherson recommends *Paramedic: On the Front Lines of Med-* *icine,* a memoir by Peter Canning: "Peter Canning is a former student from both Virginia and the Iowa Writers' Workshop. His book is an excellently written account of the lifesaving roles played by paramedics in an increasingly dangerous world. I might add that Peter is from a privileged background, was a speechwriter for the governor of Connecticut, but grew disillusioned with politics. As an alternative, he has decided to put his own life, instead of glowing words, on the line. His book deserves the broadest possible audience." (Fawcett Columbine)

Christopher Tilghman recommends *The Mirror,* a novel by Lynn Freed: "Lynn Freed pulls off a stunning tour de force in this flawless life story of a woman in South Africa after World War I. Please, read this book." (Crown)

Dan Wakefield recommends *The Collected Fiction of Bruce Jay Friedman*, stories by Bruce Jay Friedman: "One of the funniest writers of our time, the first American master of black humor fiction, he's collected his best stories in one volume. 'Brazzaville Teenager' is the best thing since Ring Lardner." (Donald I. Fine)

EDITORS' CORNER

*New Books by
Our Advisory Editors*

Frank Bidart, *Desire*, poems: Bidart's long-awaited new collection—his first book since *In the Western Night: Collected Poems 1965–90*—contains some of his most luminous and intimate work to date. The first half include poems about the art of writing, Eros, and the desolations and mirror of history (in a narrative based on Tacitus). The second half goes into even more ambitious territory, with 'The Second Hour of the Night' serving as a seductive meditation on the illusion of will. (Farrar, Straus & Giroux)

Fanny Howe, *One Crossed Out*, poems: The unforgettable voice of many of these poems belongs to May, a homeless woman, the one crossed out. The swirling language conveys a complex consciousness, bridging wisdom and madness, to deliver a searing statement on what it means to be excised from society. (Graywolf)

Marie Howe, *What the Living Do*, poems: Howe's powerful, much-anticipated second collection gives us stories of childhood, its thicket of sex and sorrow and joy, of boys and girls growing into men and women, and of a beloved brother who in his dying offered lessons on how to be most alive. (Norton)

Dan Wakefield, *Going All the Way*, a novel: First published in 1970, this coming-of-age novel of the 1950's, described as "The Midwestern *Catcher in the Rye*," has been reprinted in a new edition with a foreword by Kurt Vonnegut. A film based on Wakefield's own adaptation was released this past fall. (Indiana)

POSTSCRIPTS

ZACHARIS AWARD *Ploughshares* and Emerson College are pleased to present Carolyn Ferrell with the seventh annual John C. Zacharis First Book Award for her collection of stories, *Don't Erase Me,* which was published this summer by Houghton Mifflin. The $1,500 award—which is funded by Emerson College and named after the college's former president—honors the best debut book published by a *Ploughshares* writer, alternating annually between fiction and poetry.

Carolyn Ferrell, who is thirty-five, was born in Brooklyn and raised on Long Island. She started writing early—at the age of six, in fact. "I began to compile my rhyming (and often terrible) poems into a notebook, then went on to stories," she says. "I was obsessed with spelling as a child. I once had an argument with my first-grade teacher over a word. I was convinced the word was 'pizza' because I knew 'pizza' had a *p* and an *i* and a *z* in it. We argued for a long time. My teacher tried in vain to explain to me that it could be a different word. It was actually 'prize.' It wasn't until I reached the fourth grade and was introduced to the word 'appreciate' that the world of elusive spellings finally hit me with full, and sometimes devastating, force."

Eventually, Ferrell conquered and embraced the vagaries of language, and she attended Sarah Lawrence College for a degree in creative writing. She took classes with Allan Gurganus and Grace Paley, and, after graduating in 1984, she lived in Germany for four years—first through exchange programs to study German literature, then on a Fulbright scholarship to work as a high school teaching assistant. An accomplished violinist, Ferrell was also a member of several orchestras in Germany, including the Berlin Sibelius Orchester and the Brandenburgisches Kammerorchester. In 1988, she returned to the U.S. and began teaching adult literacy in Manhattan and then in the South Bronx, where she also directed a family literacy project.

While enrolled in the master's program in creative writing at

City College of New York, Ferrell began submitting her stories to journals and published them in *Callaloo, The Literary Review,* and *Fiction.* In 1993, her story "Proper Library" appeared in *Ploughshares* and was then selected for *The Best American Short Stories 1994* by Tobias Wolff. The story also prompted Houghton Mifflin editor Janet Silver to call Ferrell, inquiring if she had a book manuscript. "I had only three stories to show her at the time," Ferrell remembers, "but a month later, she offered me a contract."

The finished collection, *Don't Erase Me,* features eight first-person stories, eight singular voices that incandescently mix lyricism and street patois to portray the lives of mostly poor black girls. The subjects are sometimes grave—sexuality, domestic violence, AIDS, incest—but somehow her characters carry with them an unfailing passion and hope. Ferrell says, "Originally, I'd planned for the collection to center around the story 'Wonderful Teen' and focus on a coming-of-age theme set in Cal-

Lorin Klaris

ifornia, dealing with family drama, parental strife, and race issues, among other things. But once I wrote 'Proper Library,' I decided to bring in other dimensions. I liked reading the black/interracial/overweight girl everywhere: in California, in New York, in the South Bronx, in Germany."

Ferrell gives much credit for her work to the writer Doris Jean Austin. "Before she died in 1994, she taught me a great deal about the art of writing, through conversations and in workshops of the New Renaissance Writers, a black writers' group that she led. Her perception of good writing and the questions writers must ask themselves as they perfect their craft influenced me profoundly."

Ferrell is currently working on a novel that takes on Long Island in the seventies and eighties, with the teenaged narrator trying to make sense of the cultural blends and divisions in her life as historical and political events intrude with strange, resilient agency. In addition, Ferrell teaches creative writing at Sarah Lawrence and is finishing her Ph.D. in English at City University of New York. She and her husband, the psychologist Linwood Lewis, who also teaches at Sarah Lawrence, are expecting their first child in January.

The Zacharis First Book Award was inaugurated in 1991. The past winners are: Kevin Young for *Most Way Home;* Debra Spark for *Coconuts for the Saint;* Tony Hoagland for *Sweet Ruin;* Jessica Treadway for *Absent Without Leave;* Allison Joseph for *What Keeps Us Here;* and David Wong Louie for *The Pangs of Love.* The award is nominated by the advisory editors of *Ploughshares,* with founding editor DeWitt Henry acting as the final judge. There is no formal application process; all writers who have been published in *Ploughshares* are eligible, and should simply direct two copies of their first book to our office.

LAUGHLIN AWARD Tony Hoagland, a frequent contributor to *Ploughshares* and the 1994 winner of the Zacharis Award, has received the 1997 James Laughlin Award from the Academy of American Poets for his second collection of poems, *Donkey Gospel,* which will be published in April 1998 by Graywolf Press.

LAMBDA LITERARY AWARD Robin Becker has won the ninth annual Lambda Literary Award for Lesbian Poetry for her collection *All-American Girl,* which was issued by the University of Pittsburgh Press.

TRUSTEES We would like to recognize our trustees for their continuing support and assistance: Marillyn Zacharis, Jacqueline Liebergott, DeWitt Henry, Carol Houck Smith, Charles J. Beard, Frank Bidart, S. James Coppersmith, Elaine Markson, James Alan McPherson, and John Skoyles.

CONTRIBUTORS' NOTES

JULIE AGOOS is the author of *Above the Land* (Yale, 1987), which was selected by James Merrill for the Yale Series of Younger Poets, and *Calendar Year* (Sheep Meadow, 1997). She is Associate Professor of English at Brooklyn College/CUNY.

ROBIN BECKER's fourth collection of poems, *All-American Girl*, won the Lambda Literary Award in Lesbian Poetry. In 1995–96, she received a fellowship from the Bunting Institute of Radcliffe College. She is currently an associate professor at Pennsylvania State University, where she teaches in the M.F.A. program and serves as Poetry Editor for *The Women's Review of Books*.

MOLLY BENDALL's collection of poems, *After Estrangement*, was a winner in the Peregrine Smith Poetry Series and was published by Gibbs Smith in 1992. She currently teaches at the University of Southern California.

HOLLY ST. JOHN BERGON is a poet and teacher who lives in the Hudson Valley of New York and the San Juan Mountains of Colorado. She has lived and traveled in Mexico, Spain, and, most recently, England. Her work has appeared in *Pequod, Sequoia,* and *College English*. She is currently teaching at Dutchess Community College in Poughkeepsie, New York, and is married to the novelist Frank Bergon.

CHANA BLOCH directs the creative writing program at Mills College. Her books include the poetry collections *The Past Keeps Changing* and *The Secrets of the Tribe*, as well as translations of Yehuda Amichai, Dahlia Ravikovitch, and *The Song of Songs*. New poems of hers appear in *The Atlantic Monthly, The Marlboro Review, The New Yorker, Poetry, Salmagundi,* and *The Threepenny Review*.

JODY BOLZ is a poet and essayist who teaches at George Washington University. Her work has appeared recently in such publications as *The Indiana Review, River Styx, Poet Lore, Sonora Review,* and the anthology *Her Face in the Mirror* (Beacon).

PEG BOYERS is Executive Editor of *Salmagundi*. Her new poems are forthcoming in *The Paris Review* and other magazines.

KURT BROWN founded the Aspen Writers' Conference and Writers' Conferences & Festivals. He is the editor of *The True Subject, Writing It Down for James,* and *Facing the Lion,* which gather outstanding lectures from conferences. He is also the editor of *Drive, They Said: Poems about Americans and Their Cars* and the co-editor, with his wife, the poet Laure-Anne Bosselaar, of *Night Out: Poems about Hotels, Motels, Restaurants & Bars*. His first full-length collection of poems will be published by Four Way Books in 1999.

RICHARD CECIL has published two collections of poems, *Einstein's Brain* and *Alcatraz*. He teaches in the English department and the honors division at Indiana University, Bloomington.

ANN CHOI studies Korean literature at UCLA and is a former Stegner Fellow in Poetry at Stanford University. She lives in Los Angeles.

MICHAEL COLLIER's most recent book of poems is *The Neighbor* (Chicago). The editor of *The Wesleyan Tradition: Four Decades of American Poetry,* he teaches at the University of Maryland and directs the Bread Loaf Writers' Conference.

KATHRYN DAVIS's most recent novel, *Hell,* will be published this winter by The Ecco Press. She teaches at Skidmore College and lives in Vermont with her husband and daughter.

STUART DYBEK is the author of three books. He currently teaches at Western Michigan University.

KAREN FISH has published two books, *The Cedar Canoe* and *What Is Beyond Us.* "Another Republic" is from a recently completed manuscript entitled *The Nights of Knowing.* Currently she teaches at Loyola College in Maryland and is at work on a novel.

NICK FLYNN's last appearance in *Ploughshares* was in 1992 in the "Emerging Writers" issue edited by Christopher Tilghman and Marie Howe. He received his master's degree from NYU, and his manuscript of poems, *Some Ether,* was a finalist for both the Walt Whitman Award and the National Poetry Series. He lives in Brooklyn and works for Columbia University's Writing Project.

JONATHAN GALASSI's translation of Eugenio Montale's *Collected Poems 1916–1956* will be published by Farrar, Straus & Giroux in 1998.

SANDRA M. GILBERT's most recent collection of poems is *Ghost Volcano* (Norton), which won the Paterson Prize for 1995. Other recent publications include *Wrongful Death: A Memoir* (Norton) and, with Susan Gubar, *Masterpiece Theater: An Academic Melodrama* and the second edition of *The Norton Anthology of Literature by Women.* She teaches at the University of California, Davis.

JODY GLADDING lives in East Calais, Vermont. Her book, *Stone Crop,* appeared in the Yale Younger Poets Series in 1993. The poems in this issue are drawn in part from *The Medieval Health Handbook,* a compilation of plates from fourteenth-century illuminated manuscripts.

BARRY GOLDENSOHN is the author of *St. Venus Eve, Uncarving the Block, The Marrano,* and *Dance Music,* and he is completing another book of poems tentatively called *The Work of Ending.* His poems and essays have appeared in *Salmagundi, Poetry, The Yale Review, The New Republic, Ploughshares,* and elsewhere. He teaches at Skidmore College.

LORRIE GOLDENSOHN has published two poetry collections, *The Tether* and *Dreamwork.* She is also the author of *Elizabeth Bishop: The Biography of a Poetry.*

DANIEL GUTSTEIN has poetry forthcoming in *The American Scholar, Poet Lore,* and *The Midwest Quarterly.* He has also published work in *Fiction.* A former economist, farmhand, and tae kwon do instructor, he has taught creative writing at two universities. He is at work on a collection of poems entitled *Undoing.*

TONY HOAGLAND's first collection of poems, *Sweet Ruin* (Wisconsin), won the Brittingham Prize in Poetry and the John C. Zacharis First Book Award from *Ploughshares*. His second collection, *Donkey Gospel*, which is forthcoming from Graywolf Press in April, won the James Laughlin Award this past fall. He teaches at New Mexico State University and Warren Wilson College.

JOYCE JOHNSON's published books include *Bad Connections, In the Night Cafe, What Lisa Knew*, and a memoir, *Minor Characters*, which won a National Book Critics Circle Award in 1983. She teaches in the M.F.A. program at Columbia University.

HETTIE JONES is the author of *How I Became Hettie Jones*, a memoir of the Beat scene, as well as award-winning books for children and young adults. Her poetry collection, *Drive*, is just out from Hanging Loose Press. She teaches in New York at Parsons and the 92nd Street Y.

LILY KING lives in Cambridge, Massachusetts. She recently completed a novel called *Plaire*.

PHILIP LEVINE's most recent collection of new poems, *The Simple Truth* (Knopf), won the Pulitzer Prize for poetry in 1995.

JON LOOMIS currently directs the Summer Workshops at the Fine Arts Work Center in Provincetown. His poems have appeared in *Poetry, Field, The Gettysburg Review, The Iowa Review, The North American Review*, and other journals. His first book, *Vanitas Motel*, won the *Field* Poetry Prize and is due out from Oberlin College Press in December 1997.

DAVID MAMET's plays include *Oleanna; Glengarry Glen Ross*, which won the Pulitzer Prize and the New York Drama Critics Circle Award in 1984; *American Buffalo;* and *The Cryptogram*, a 1995 Obie Award winner. His films include *The Postman Always Rings Twice, The Verdict, The Untouchables*, and *The Edge*. He is also the author of three children's books, four volumes of essays, a collection of poems, and a novel.

GAIL MAZUR is the author of three poetry collections, most recently *The Common* (Chicago). She is the founding director of the Blacksmith House Poetry Series in Cambridge and is 1997–98 Poet-in-Residence at Emerson College. In 1996–97, she was the Fellow in Poetry at the Bunting Institute at Radcliffe College.

DAVID MCALEAVEY has taught creative writing and literature at George Washington University since 1974. His fourth and most recent book of poems is *Holding Obsidian* (Washington Writers', 1985). He has published in numerous magazines, including *Poetry, The Georgia Review*, and *The Antioch Review*. Last winter, he was an exchange fellow from the Virginia Center for the Creative Arts to the Schloss Wiepersdorf colony near Berlin, Germany.

GARDNER MCFALL is the author of *The Pilot's Daughter* (Time Being, 1996). Her poems have appeared previously in *Ploughshares*, as well as in *The Nation, The Paris Review, The New Yorker*, and elsewhere. She teaches literature at The Cooper Union in New York City.

NORA MITCHELL is the author of two collections of poems, *Proofreading the Histories* (1996) and *Your Skin Is a Country* (1988), both from Alice James Books. Her poems have appeared in *Ploughshares, Calyx, College English, Hanging Loose, Radical America,* and *Sojourner,* among other magazines. She directs the M.F.A. program at Goddard College.

EUGENIO MONTALE (1896–1981) is generally considered one of the greatest Italian poets of the twentieth century. He received the Nobel Prize in Literature in 1976.

CAROL MUSKE's two new books are *An Octave Above Thunder: New and Selected Poems* (Penguin) and *Women and Poetry: Truth, Autobiography and the Shape of the Self* (Poets on Poetry Series, Michigan). She is Professor of English at the University of Southern California, where she teaches creative writing.

PAUL NELSON lives in Machiasport, Maine. His books are *Cargo* (Stonewall), *Average Nights* (L'Epervier), *Days Off* (Virginia), and *The Hard Shapes of Paradise* (Alabama). A new book, *Cold Watch,* is ready for publication. Recent poems appear in *The Ohio Review, Salmagundi, River Styx, Willow Springs,* and *The Sandhills Review.*

JOSIP NOVAKOVICH teaches at the University of Cincinnati. Graywolf Press published his collection of stories, *Yolk,* and his collection of essays, *Apricots from Chernobyl,* and will be releasing his new collection of stories, *Salvation and Other Disasters,* this coming spring.

GREGORY ORR's most recent collection is *City of Salt* (Pittsburgh, 1995). His first book, *Burning the Empty Nests,* has just been reissued by Carnegie-Mellon University Press. He is the co-editor, with Ellen Bryant Voigt, of the essay collection *Poets Teaching Poets: Self and the World* (Michigan, 1996). He teaches at the University of Virginia and is completing a memoir and a book about lyric poetry and survival.

JOYCE PESEROFF's two books of poems are *The Hardness Scale* (Alice James) and *A Dog in the Lifeboat* (Carnegie-Mellon). She is currently Visiting Professor and Poet-in-Residence at the University of Massachusetts, Boston.

STANLEY PLUMLY's most recent book of poems, *The Marriage in the Trees,* appeared last spring from The Ecco Press. He currently teaches at the University of Maryland.

JACK PULASKI is the author of *The St. Veronica Gig Stories.* His stories have appeared in various magazines and anthologies, including *The Ploughshares Reader* and *The Pushcart Prize.* "Laura Providencia in the New World" is from a book that he expects to complete shortly.

MARK RUDMAN is a poet, essayist, and translator. His recent books include a long poem, *Rider,* which received the National Book Critics Circle Award in Poetry for 1994; a book of essays, *Realm of Unknowing: Meditations on Art, Suicide, and Other Transformations* (1995); and *The Millennium Hotel* (1996)—all three with Wesleyan University Press. He has recently completed *Provoked in Venice,* the third volume of his trilogy.

MARY JO SALTER is the author of three volumes of poetry, most recently *Sunday Skaters* (Knopf, 1994). She is also a co-editor of the fourth edition of *The Norton Anthology of Poetry* (1996). She teaches at Mount Holyoke College.

LLOYD SCHWARTZ is the director of the creative writing program at the University of Massachusetts, Boston, and a regular commentator on NPR's "Fresh Air." For his articles on classical music in *The Boston Phoenix,* he received the 1994 Pulitzer Prize for criticism. His most recent book of poems is *Goodnight, Gracie.*

LAURIE SHECK's most recent book of poems, *The Willow Grove* (Knopf, 1996), was a finalist for the Pulitzer Prize. She currently teaches at Princeton University.

TOM SLEIGH is the author of three books of poetry: *After One* (Houghton Mifflin, 1983), *Waking* (Chicago, 1990), and *The Chain* (Chicago, 1996). His fourth book, *The Dreamhouse,* will appear in 1999.

ELIZABETH SPIRES's most recent book of poems is *Worldling* (Norton, 1995). A Whiting Award recipient in 1996, she lives in Baltimore and teaches at Goucher College. Recently, she finished editing *The Instant of Knowing* (Michigan), a collection of Josephine Jacobsen's occasional prose.

PHILIP ST. CLAIR teaches at the University of Kentucky at Ashland. His latest book, *Acid Creek,* was published in 1997 by Bottom Dog Press. He was awarded an NEA fellowship in 1994 and the Bullis Prize from *Poetry Northwest* in 1986.

DAVID ST. JOHN is the author of five collections of poetry, most recently *Study for the World's Body: New and Selected Poems* (HarperCollins, 1994), which was nominated for the National Book Award. He has also published a collection of prose, *Where the Angels Come Toward Us: Selected Essays, Reviews, and Interviews* (1995).

MAURA STANTON's new book of poetry, *Life Among the Trolls,* will be published by Carnegie-Mellon in 1998. She teaches at Indiana University, Bloomington.

RUTH STONE's eight books include *Simplicity* (1995) and *Ordinary Words* (forthcoming in the fall of 1998), both from Paris Press. A collection of essays on her work by eighteen fellow poets and scholars, *The House Is Made of Poetry,* was recently published by Southern Illinois University Press.

CHASE TWICHELL's most recent book is *The Ghost of Eden* (Ontario, 1994). A new book, *The Snow Watcher,* is forthcoming from Ontario Review Press in 1998. She teaches in the M.F.A. program at Goddard College.

SUSAN WALP is represented by the Fischbach Gallery in New York City, where she exhibits regularly. Her most recent solo exhibition was in August 1997 in Montecastello di Vibio, Italy, where she spent part of the summer on the painting faculty for the International School of Art. She has received fellowships from the NEA and the New York Creative Arts Public Service Program. She lives in Washington, Vermont, and teaches at Vermont College of Norwich University.

KEVIN YOUNG's first book, *Most Way Home* (William Morrow, 1995) was a National Poetry Series winner and also won the 1996 John C. Zacharis First Book Award from *Ploughshares.* "Satchmo" is taken from a series inspired by the late painter Jean-Michel Basquiat; other poems have appeared or are forthcoming in

The New Yorker, The Kenyon Review, Callaloo, and *DoubleTake,* as well as in *Two Cents,* a traveling exhibit and catalogue. He is currently an assistant professor at the University of Georgia.

~

SUBSCRIBERS Please feel free to contact us via e-mail with address changes (the post office usually will not forward journals) or any problems with your subscription. Our e-mail address is: pshares@emerson.edu. Also, please note that on occasion we exchange mailing lists with other literary magazines and organizations. If you would like your name excluded from these exchanges, simply send us an e-mail message or a letter stating so.

SUBMISSION POLICIES *Ploughshares* is published three times a year: usually mixed issues of poetry and fiction in the Spring and Winter and a fiction issue in the Fall, with each guest-edited by a different writer. We welcome unsolicited manuscripts from August 1 to March 31 (postmark dates). All submissions sent from April to July are returned unread. In the past, guest editors often announced specific themes for issues, but we have revised our editorial policies and no longer restrict submissions to thematic topics. Submit your work at any time during our reading period; if a manuscript is not timely for one issue, it will be considered for another. Send one prose piece and/or one to three poems at a time (mail genres separately). Poems should be individually typed either single- or double-spaced on one side of the page. Prose should be typed double-spaced on one side and be no longer than twenty-five pages. Although we look primarily for short stories, we occasionally publish personal essays/memoirs. Novel excerpts are acceptable if self-contained. Unsolicited book reviews and criticism are not considered. Please do not send multiple submissions of the same genre, and do not send another manuscript until you hear about the first. Additional submissions will be returned unread. No more than a total of three submissions per reading period, please. Mail your manuscript in a page-size manila envelope, your full name and address written on the outside, to the "Fiction Editor," "Poetry Editor," or "Nonfiction Editor." Unsolicited work sent directly to a guest editor's home or office will be ignored and discarded; guest editors are formally instructed not to read such work. All manuscripts and correspondence regarding submissions should be accompanied by a self-addressed, stamped envelope (S.A.S.E.) for a response. Expect three to five months for a decision. Do not query us until five months have passed, and if you do, please write to us, including an S.A.S.E. and indicating the postmark date of submission, instead of calling. Simultaneous submissions are amenable as long as they are indicated as such and we are notified immediately upon acceptance elsewhere. We cannot accommodate revisions, changes of return address, or forgotten S.A.S.E.'s after the fact. We do not reprint previously published work. Translations are welcome if permission has been granted. We cannot be responsible for delay, loss, or damage. Payment is upon publication: $25/printed page, $50 minimum per title, $250 maximum per author, with two copies of the issue and a one-year subscription.

Ploughshares Donors

With great gratitude, we would like to acknowledge the following readers who generously made donations to *Ploughshares* during our 1997 fund-raising campaign.

Anonymous (7)
William Alfred
Sharon Anson
Ann Barnard
Miles and Donna Benedict
Margi Berger
Rebecca Boyd
Pierce A. Brennan
Robert Brooks
Scott Buck
Jean Burden
Ron Carroll
James Carroll and
  Alexandra Marshall
Johanna Cinader
Richard Concannon
Miles A. Coon
Wyn Cooper
Mary Lynn H. Dickson
Paula Eder
Barbara Erdle
Charles C. Foster
Marion H. Freeman
Charles Glass
Michael Glenn
Rachel Goldstein
Ethan Hauser
E. M. Higgins
Nathaniel C. Hutner
Gish Jen
X. J. Kennedy
Alice Kenner

Maxine Kumin
Sophia Leopold
Dr. Harold R. Lohr
Alice Mattison
Fiona McCrae
Videen Marna McGaughey
Devon McNamara
Bob Meeks
Kenneth Mintz
Judith H. Montgomery
Mollie Lee Pryor
Sheila Roark
Roger Sale
Steven Schwartz
Tammy J. Senk
Carol Houck Smith
Gary Soto
Debra Spark
Maura Stanton
Tree Swenson
Wayne and Carole Tippit
Eileen Tobin
Joanne Trafton
Valorie M. Vejvoda
Gale Ward
Miriam M. Wexler
Susan Wheeler
Annelie Wilde
Rodney Wittwer and
  Deborah Parker
Ria Young

INDEX TO VOLUME XXIII

Ploughshares · A Journal of New Writing · 1997

BOOK REVIEWS

BENNINGTON WRITING SEMINARS

MFA in Writing and Literature
Two-Year Low-Residency Program

A. BLAKE GARDNER

FICTION
NONFICTION
POETRY

Jane Kenyon Poetry Scholarship available
For more information contact:
Writing Seminars
Box PL
Bennington College
Bennington, VT 05201
802-442-5401 ext. 4452, Fax 802-442-6164

THE BIRD ARTIST
HOWARD NORMAN

"Classic.... All that is splendid and spectacular in the book is simply light, magically employed, to seek out what is real."
—Richard Eder, *The Los Angeles Times Book Review*

"Bewitching...glows like a nightlight in the reader's mind."—Michiko Kakutani, *The New York Times*

"Completely original and compelling...written with great intelligence, wit and clarity."
—Anne Whitehouse, *The Boston Sunday Globe*

MUSIC MINUS ONE
JANE SHORE

THE NATIONAL BOOK CRITICS CIRCLE AWARD FOR POETRY FINALIST

"Impressive.... A seamless arc of personal history, both artful and accessible."
—Gardner McFall, *The New York Times Book Review*

"Reading her poetry is like having coffee with a talkative relative full of stories from the past. Shore has a wonderful knack for narrative and spins out her tales with moving, compelling richness."—*Library Journal*

"A deftly focused memoir...[Jane Shore's] language attains a transparency that marks her gift for being objective and heartfelt at the same time."—Jonathan Aaron, *The Boston Sunday Globe*

Princeton University Press
congratulates Robert Pinsky
on his selection as
U.S. Poet Laureate

Princeton University Press published Robert Pinsky's first books and we are pleased that they remain available in bookstores throughout the country. To view samples from each book below, please visit our website: pup.princeton.edu.

© Sigrid Estrada

Sadness And Happiness

"Remarkable . . . What [these poems] are attempting is important: nothing less than the recovery for language of a whole domain of mute and familiar experience."
—Hugh Kenner, *The Los Angeles Times Book Review*
Paper $9.95 ISBN 0-691-01322-5

An Explanation of America

"[An] ambitious and immensely likable long poem . . . a poem which—a rare thing—seems to combine intimacy and authority."
—David Kalstone, *The New York Times Book Review*

"Wise and compassionate. . . . It is one of the most readable long poems in recent memory, graspable by all."—Kenneth Funsten, *The Los Angeles Times*
Paper $9.95 ISBN 0-691-01360-8

The Situation of Poetry
Contemporary Poetry and Its Traditions

"The mind at work in *The Situation of Poetry* is lively, fresh, and critical without being obsessed by the rigor of criticism. [Pinsky's] comments are brief, vivid, distinct . . . and his taste is excellent."
—Denis Donoghue, *The New York Times Book Review*

"No one can read Pinsky's writing without being provoked to thought."
—Helen Vendler, *The Nation*

Paper $14.95 ISBN 0-691-01352-7

Princeton University Press
AVAILABLE AT FINE BOOKSTORES OR DIRECTLY FROM THE PUBLISHER: 800-777-4726
VISIT OUR WEBSITE: PUP.PRINCETON.EDU

NEW FROM GRAYWOLF PRESS

The Outermost Dream: Literary Sketches
WILLIAM MAXWELL
Paperback, $12.95 (1-55597-264-0)

Reviewing biographies, memoirs, diaries, and correspondence, Maxwell offers keen insights into the lives of fascinating individuals including such literary luminaries as Virginia Woolf, Lord Byron, and E.B. White.

From the Devotions
CARL PHILLIPS
Paperback, $12.95 (1-55597-263-2)

Award-winning poet Carl Phillips takes us even further into that dangerous space he has already made his own, where body and soul—ever restless—come explosively together.

One Crossed Out
FANNY HOWE
Paperback, $12.95 (1-55597-259-4)

"Fanny Howe is a sly, wicked poet, always shifting between the social, the political, as well as the linguistic and literary concerns of an artist always writing from the cutting edge. *One Crossed Out* is a thrilling book of poetry by a poet in total control of her craft and her voice." *Quincy Troupe*

A Four-Sided Bed
ELIZABETH SEARLE
Paperback, $14.00 (1-55597-265-9)

Searle's debut novel explores gender identity and the sexual boundaries of friendship and love through the uninhibited passion of a relationship with multiple partners. This sexy, four-sided love story is unique to our gender-testing times.

Night Talk

ELIZABETH COX

Hardcover, $23.95 (1-55597-267-5)

Set in the Deep South during the Civil Rights years, this novel explores the unlikely friendship between two girls, one black and one white. Growing up in the same house, they experience a world apart from the one outside their door. Taking refuge in their candid nighttime conversations, Evie and Janey Louise form a powerful bond strong enough to withstand the perils of family tragedy, rape, and racial injustice.

Raised in Captivity:
Why Does America Fail Its Children?

LUCIA HODGSON

Hardcover, $23.95 (1-55597-261-6)

Hodgson strips away the hype to reveal America's self-deception about children's realities. Her groundbreaking book sets the stage for a new dialogue about how to ensure that children are protected, provided for, and guaranteed basic civil rights.

Otherwise: New and Selected Poems

JANE KENYON

Now Available in Paperback, $16.00 (1-55597-266-7)

"Her words, with their quiet, rapt force, their pensiveness and wit, come to us from natural speech, from the Bible and hymns, from which she derived the singular psalmlike music that is hers alone." *The New York Times Book Review*

GRAYWOLF PRESS
2402 University Avenue, Suite 203
St. Paul, MN 55114
(612) 641-0077 / Fax: (612) 641-0036
www.graywolfpress.org

best (bĕst) *adj.* 1. Surpassing all others in quality.
2. **Prize Stories 1997** and **The Anchor Essay Annual 1997.**

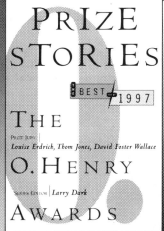

Miami University
OXFORD, OHIO
Press

KISSES
Steve Orlen

73 pp.
$19.95 cloth ISBN 1-881163-20-2
$11.95 paper ISBN 1-881163-21-0

Orlen is a wonderful poet and one of the best practitioners of free verse writing today. The sounds of his poems bang and glide. Most fine poetry strikes the mind and heart. This is true of Orlen as well, but his poems also strike the ear. They feel good in the mouth. —Stephen Dobyns

*Orlen's **Bridge of Sighs**, like Eliot's "Prufrock," is filled with many human voices, but they are the voices around us, the recognizable voices of people we know too well. . . . He builds from memory, from old photographs, mental snapshots of the past, and he knows where to break a line and also how to break your heart.*
—Mark Hillringhouse in *The Literary Review*

WHAT WIND WILL DO
Debra Bruce

59 pp.
$19.95 cloth ISBN 1-881163-18-0
$11.95 paper ISBN 1-881163-19-9

I admire Debra Bruce's adroit use of form. Through it, paradoxically, she has acquired the freedom to confront subjects that range from cancer to infertility and she does so with grace. —Maxine Kumin

Along with such poets as Marilyn Hacker, Jane Kenyon, and Mary Oliver, Bruce has given us another woman's voice we have to listen to!
—Julia Alvarez

LONG DISTANCE
Aleda Shirley

77 pp.
$19.95 cloth ISBN 1-881163-16-4
$11.95 paper ISBN 1-881163-17-2

The idea that "America may always be more a passage than a place" is explored with kaleidoscopic resonance and cut-glass clarity in this moving second collection by Mississippi poet Shirley.... Throughout, both time and space are evocatively shape-shifting dimensions.... Shirley's measured lyric language and seamless craftsmanship reveal the offroad intimacies and profundities of the American landscape.
—*Publishers Weekly* (starred review)

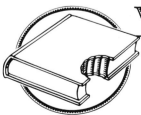

Ploughshares

a literary adventure

Known for its compelling fiction and poetry, *Ploughshares* is widely regarded as one of America's most influential literary journals. Each issue is guest-edited by a different writer for a fresh, provocative slant—exploring personal visions, aesthetics, and literary circles—and contributors include both well-known and emerging writers. In fact, *Ploughshares* has become a premier proving ground for new talent, showcasing the early works of Sue Miller, Mona Simpson, Robert Pinsky, and countless others. Past guest editors include Richard Ford, Derek Walcott, Tobias Wolff, Carolyn Forché, and Rosellen Brown. This unique editorial format has made *Ploughshares,* in effect, into a dynamic anthology series—one that has established a tradition of quality and prescience. *Ploughshares* is published in quality trade paperback in April, August, and December: usually a fiction issue in the Fall and mixed issues of poetry and fiction in the Spring and Winter. Inside each issue, you'll find not only great new stories and poems, but also a profile on the guest editor, book reviews, and miscellaneous notes about *Ploughshares,* its writers, and the literary world. Subscribe today.

Sample *Ploughshares* on the Web: http://www.emerson.edu/ploughshares

---